*Jung's Quest
for Wholeness*

Jung's Quest
for Wholeness

A Religious and Historical Perspective

Curtis D. Smith

State University of New York Press

Published by
State University of New York Press, Albany

©1990 State University of New York

For information, address State University of New York
Press, State University Plaza, Albany, N.Y., 12246

Library of Congress Cataloging-in-Publication Data

Smith, Curtis D., 1951-
   Jung's quest for wholeness : a religious and historical
perspective / Curtis D. Smith.
      p.   cm.
   Bibliography: p.
   Includes index.
   ISBN 0-7914-0237-1. — ISBN 0-7914-0238-X (pbk.)
   1. Psychoanalysis and religion—History.   2. Psychology,
Religious—History.   3. Jung, C. G. (Carl Gustav), 1875-1961.
   I. Title.
BF175.4.R44S65   1990   89-11313
150.19′54—dc20   CIP

10   9   8   7   6   5   4   3   2   1

Contents

I knew that in finding the mandala
as an expression of the self I had
attained what was for me the ultimate.
Perhaps someone else knows more,
but not I.

Jung
Memories, Dreams, Reflections

Acknowledgments

I want to express my appreciation to The University of Iowa
School of Religion and its director, Dr. John Boyle, for making
the writing of this work possible. In particular, I wish to thank
Professor David Belgum who contributed much time and effort
in reading through the text. Likewise, Dr. George Paterson read
the manuscript at various stages, and offered many valuable
suggestions for its improvement. I am grateful to Professor W.
Pachow for his encouragement and advice while I was working
on the manuscript. A special thanks goes to Professor Robert
Baird for his time and methodological insights that sharpened
the focus of this work. I am also indebted to Dr. Lauralee
Rockwell for her generous help and support. Ronald Jensen
deserves special mention for the critical perspective he contributed to the project at a number of key stages in its development.
Dr. Timothy Hunt and Dr. James Foard, although not directly
involved in this work, nonetheless provided the foundation that
allowed me to undertake and complete this project. While I am
grateful to all those mentioned above for their contributions,
any errors remain solely my responsibility. And finally, this
volume is dedicated to my parents and sister for all their love
and kindness throughout the years.

Introduction

When reading the *Collected Works* of the Swiss psychiatrist Carl Gustav Jung, one encounters a seemingly endless array of topics. Beginning with his studies in occult phenomena, through his work on the word association experiment, dementia praecox, and his involvement and subsequent break with Sigmund Freud, Jung spent the first half of his life attempting to develop a theory of the human personality. The second half of his life was no less productive as he further elaborated and extended his thought into a variety of cultural areas: mythology, symbolism, alchemy, Eastern and Western religions, psychotherapy, and modernity all fell within the domain of his research.

Thus anyone studying Jung's thought must decide on which aspect of his system to focus, and what questions to ask of the data. Theologians, for example, have used Jung's writings to provide psychological insight into aspects of Christian doctrine.[1] Similarly, psychologists have turned to Jung's writings on therapy to explain various mental disorders, while still other scholars have employed Jung's archetypal theories to interpret literary works.[2] On the other hand, there are those working within the Jungian tradition whose goal is to further that tradition by demonstrating the validity and relevancy of Jung's theories for contemporary society.[3]

Likewise, as a historian of religions, I bring to this study a particular set of questions designed to limit the area of my research. Contrary to those approaches described above, my aim is neither the use of Jung's theories as a hermeneutical tool,

1

nor the propagation of the Jungian tradition. Rather, by approaching Jung's thought via the religio-historical method, I will examine the proposed *religious goal* or "ultimate concern" of his psychotherapeutic system.[4]

It should be noted that my definition of religion as ultimate concern functions as a stipulative definition, not a real one. Briefly, a real definition posits an essence to the particular object defined, while a stipulative definition does not claim to define the essence of a thing. It only claims that a particular word, in a given study, will be used in a specified way. This is a crucial point when dealing with an ambiguous word like "religion." Rather than proceed as if everyone knows what the essence of religion is, a stipulative definition makes it clear from the start how the term "religion" will be used. By defining "religion" as ultimate concern, then, I mean that which is more important to a person than anything else in the universe. Although I am not suggesting that this is the only or true definition of religion, one would be hard pressed to assert that the question of ultimacy is not one of the most important questions that could be asked of a body of thought.[5]

Specifically, in the context of this study, I will be seeking to find what Jung envisioned as the ultimate or highest goal of human existence. But more than simply identifying the religious goal of Jung's psychotherapeutic system, I will also be asking a number of historical questions: "When did Jung formulate his ultimate concern, and to what extent did it change over time?" My aim here is to describe the evolution of Jung's ultimate concern throughout his theoretical writings, particularly his *Collected Works*. It is precisely this combination of religio-historical concerns which makes this approach to Jung's thought unique.

This is, however, not to deny the validity of other methods and approaches to Jung's thought. A review of the secondary literature reveals the presence of numerous religious and historical studies of Jung's work, each providing valid insights into different aspects of his thought. Generally speaking, though, the available historical studies do not focus specifically on the religious goal of his system, but on the development of his ideas in general. On the other hand, the concerns of those studies attempting a religious analysis of Jung's system, are, for the most part, not of a historical nature. Rather, the majority of these studies focus on Jung's interpretation of religious phenomena, or compare his thought to various religious thinkers.

This study, by contrast, will describe the religious goal found within Jung's psychological system, and trace the evolution of that goal throughout his *Collected Works*. Here I want to be clear: this is not a study of Jung's views on "traditional" religion, but an examination of the religious goal of his theoretical writings. Whereas the former refers to Jung's interpretation of religious experience, the latter refers to the ultimate concern of his psychotherapeutic system. This is a crucial distinction which previous studies have not yet fully explored.

Such an investigation will lead us to see that the religious goal of Jung's work can best be described as the quest for human wholeness. Psychologically viewed, wholeness is symbolized by the archetype of the self. The search for self-realization or wholeness is known as the way of individuation, and is the main goal of the therapeutic process. In and of itself this insight is hardly novel. What I intend to demonstrate, therefore, is that the individuation of the self has implications that extend far beyond the purely therapeutic realm. More precisely, by therapeutic I mean the removal of temporary obstacles to growth. By contrast, the quest for wholeness functions as more than simply a neutral therapeutic goal, but is the religious goal of Jung's psychotherapeutic system.[6]

When this general observation is applied specifically to Jung's theoretical writings, we find there an implicit tension between his claims of therapeutic neutrality, and his tendency to make statements about the ultimate nature and purpose of human existence. In this study, therefore, I intend to show that in addition to whatever penultimate therapeutic goals Jung's system may have, it also contains a distinctly religious one. Being the main goal of life, wholeness has the potential to endow existence with ultimate meaning and value; in this sense it is the ultimate concern or religious goal of Jung's system. Thus, Jung's quest for wholeness can be characterized as a nontranscendent form of psychological ultimacy. It is nontranscendent in that the locus of ultimacy is the individual, and it is psychological in that Jung elevates the psyche and its development to a plane of absolute importance.

In the following chapters, I have divided the evolution of the religious goal of Jung's thought into three distinct phases: developmental, formative, and elaborative. A discussion of the developmental phase (1895-1913), consisting of the time prior to the creation of Jung's ultimate concern, beginning with his university studies, and ending immediately after his break with Sigmund Freud, forms the basis of part two. As we will see, during this period Jung's research interests focused on the fragmentation of the human psyche. In part three I discuss the formative years (1913-1928), during which time Jung began to consolidate the contours of his newly emerging ultimate concern. At this time we get the first full theoretical description of both his ultimate concern and pattern of ultimacy. Here Jung sought and found in his notion of the self the solution to the problem of psychic fragmentation. And finally, in part four I examine the years of elaboration (1929-1961) when Jung expanded and clarified both his ultimate concern and pattern of ultimacy. During these latter years, Jung expanded the unifying capacity of the self to include the oneness of the psychic and material realms.

One final introductory point needs to be made in order to avoid any unnecessary confusion about the nature and purpose of this study. It is important to keep in mind that this work is not intended as a comprehensive biography of Jung's life, but a study of his theoretical writings as found in his *Collected Works*. Because of that, I have avoided a detailed analysis of his life, particularly his childhood years, in favor of focusing on the evolution of his thought. Much confusion will be avoided if one keeps in mind this distinction between the real (biographical) and ideal (theoretical) levels of investigation. This distinction will be dealt with further in my description of the religio-historical method.

Part I

Methodological Considerations

Chapter One

Approach to Jung

In this chapter I present a brief biographical overview of Jung's life, followed by a discussion of those secondary sources which have helped to shape this study.[1] I have arranged these studies according to biographical, religious, and historical approaches. After discussing these studies, I review those works concerned specifically with the individuation process. And finally, I conclude chapter one with a description of the religio-historical method in order to clarify the methodological assumptions and object of this study.

BIOGRAPHICAL OVERVIEW

Carl Gustav Jung was born in Kesswil, Switzerland, 26 July 1875, where he spent the first six months of his life.[2] Jung's father, Paul Achilles Jung (1842-1896), had studied classical languages at Göttingen where he wrote his dissertation on the Arabic version of the Song of Songs.[3] After his marriage to Emile Preiswerk (1848-1923), he began his career as a country pastor at a parish in Kesswil. The Jung's had three children, the first of whom lived only a few days; Carl Gustav, the second of the three children, was born some nine years after the death of the first child.

Six months after Carl's birth the family moved to Laufen near the Rhine Falls, remaining there for three years, before moving once again, this time to Klein-Hüningen, a small village near Basel where Carl received his early education. As it turned out, Klein-Hüningen was the third and final parish for the Reverend Paul Jung. Additional contemporaneous documentation regarding the life of Carl in these early years, other than the retrospective account given in his autobiography, is scarce. Generally speaking, the impression we receive from his autobiography is that these early years were a time of conflict and loneliness for him.

His secondary education was consumed by his interest in theological and philosophical matters. Jung mentions reading the works of various philosophers and writers such as Schopenhauer and Goethe.[4] He also expresses experiencing intense personal conflict between the dreams and images of his inner world, and his childhood upbringing in Christianity. Although distrustful of the Church, he still attempted to commit himself to Christianity by preparing for his first communion. He describes how he readied himself for this event, and how his expectations rose; the actual experience, however, was flat and without meaning. This event was a major blow against any hope Jung might still have harbored for establishing a relationship with the Church. In retrospect, Jung tells what a devastating realization this was for him, of how all religious meaning was dissolved. "I had, so it seemed to me, suffered the greatest defeat of my life. The religious outlook which I imagined constituted my sole meaningful relation with the universe had disintegrated. ... "[5] But despite his disappointment, he passed his secondary school examinations in 1895, thus paving the way for his university studies.

After some hesitation, Jung chose to study medicine at the University of Basel where he registered 18 April 1895. Less than a year later his father died leaving him to care for his mother and sister, both of whom were now living in Binningen close to the medical school. There are two noteworthy facts from this period: Jung's interest in psychic phenomena, and his decision to specialize in psychiatry. The former interest came to fruition while Jung attended a number of seances given by a distant cousin. The results of his research were formulated in his doctoral dissertation and subsequently published under the title *On the Psychology and Pathology of So-called Occult Phenomena* (1902).[6]

In addition, Jung began to develop his interest in psychiatry. He mentions that while studying for his doctoral exams he came upon a book by Kraft-Ebing entitled, *Lehrbuch der Psychiatria*. At that moment, he writes, "it had become clear to me, . . . that for me the only possible goal was psychiatry."[7] Coupled with his previous courses in psychiatry, this newly emerging interest marked the culmination of his student years. Beginning with his career uncertainty in 1895, psychiatry provided the point where his varied vocational and intellectual interests could finally merge.[8] Jung was now ready to begin his study of the human psyche in earnest.

After completing his final university examinations in 1899, Jung took up residence at the Burghölzli Psychiatric Hospital in Zurich, where, under the direction of Professor Eugen Bleuler, Jung received intensive firsthand clinical experience working with severe cases of mental illness. His dissertation was published in 1902, and in the winter of that same year, after briefly studying with Pierre Janet in Paris, Jung returned to Burghölzli and married Emma Rauschenbach on 14 February 1903.

While at Burghölzli Jung began his work on the word association test, publishing a complete volume on this topic in 1906.[9] He was also given the position of First *Oberarzt* at the hospital and the title of *Privat Dozent* at the university where he taught various courses on psychiatry. During this same period, Jung began his association with the Viennese doctor, Sigmund Freud, which lasted from 1906 to 1914. For most of these years, Jung was an ardent follower and supportor of Freud's ideas. Both *The Freud/Jung Letters* and his theoretical writings during this time illustrate his involvement and commitment to the emerging psychoanalytic movement.[10]

In 1907 Jung published a major work on mental illness entitled, *The Psychology of Dementia Praecox*.[11] Two years later, he and Freud made their historic trip to America to lecture at Clark University in Massachusetts. Shortly after his return, Jung departed from Burghölzli, moved into his newly built home at Küsnacht and began his own private practice. He was also elected president of the International Psychoanalytic Association and became editor of the *Jahrbuch*, the offical psychoanalytic journal.

But by 1911 Jung was diverging more and more from Freud's theories, a fact clearly evident in a 1911/1912 work eventually published in English as *The Psychology of the Unconscious* (1916).[12] Jung subsequently resigned as editor of the *Jahrbuch* in October 1913, and as president of the International Psychoanalytic Association in April 1914. During the following five years (1914-1919) he underwent a period of intense crisis and confusion; as a means to deal with his inner turmoil, he began recording and analyzing the various psychic images that he encountered. Unfortunately, the two works in which he recorded his experiences—the *Black Book* and the *Red Book*—have not been published, although a retrospective account of this period is given in his autobiography. Jung published very little during this period.

By 1919 the intensity of his inner upheaval subsided, and in 1921 he published his well-known work, *Psychological Types*.[13] Between the years 1924 and 1926 Jung traveled to New Mexico to spend time with the Pueblo Indians and to Africa to live with a tribe on Mount Elgon. In the 1930s, as his popularity grew, he became honorary president of the German Society of Psychotherapy, president of the International Society for Psychotherapy, Professor of Psychology at the Swiss Polytechnical School in Zurich, and even lectured at Harvard, receiving the honorary degree of Doctor of Science. He then traveled to India in 1937 and received an honorary doctorate from the University of Calcutta. Oxford University likewise honored him with a doctorate in 1938.

Despite nearly dying from a heart problem in 1944, Jung slowly began writing and working again after his recovery. In 1948 the C.G Jung Institute in Zurich opened, and to this day it functions as a research and training center for those interested in becoming Jungian analysts. This was also the period of his life when Jung was most heavily involved with his alchemical researches, which culminated in 1951 with the publication of his *magnum opus, Mysterium Coniunctionis*.[14] His last two major pieces of writing include work on his autobiography and a chapter for the book *Man and His Symbols*.[15] Jung died 6 June 1961 at the age of eighty-five in his home at Küsnacht.

LITERATURE REVIEW

Biographical Studies

Although not strictly concerned with Jung's religious goal, these studies nevertheless attempt a general appraisal of Jung's quest for wholeness, and thus must be taken into consideration. Broadly viewed, there are two distinct categories of biographical writings—apologetic and critical. Barbara Hannah's biography of Jung, which views him as the wise old man possessing superior insight, is a prime example of the former.[16] Her strong pro-Jung sentiment is evident, for instance, in her positive assessment of Jung's attainment of wholeness. "But the extraordinary degree of wholeness which he attained, and the thoroughness with which every possible aspect of his life was lived, make it impossible for any book about him, even if it ran ten volumes, to portray more than a fraction of this fullness".[17]

Throughout this work, then, Jung is portrayed as a larger-than-life mythic figure having achieved an incomparable degree of self-realization. Other Jungians take a similar view of Jung's life and work. Marie-Louise von Franz and Laurens Van der Post both approach Jung's work in a normative fashion, that is, as scholars working within the Jungian tradition.[18] Although these works are useful in providing biographical data not found in Jung's autobiography, their strong pro-Jung sentiment must be taken into account.

By contrast, Paul Stern's *The Haunted Prophet* provides a critical assessment of Jung's quest for wholeness.[19] The picture we get of Jung is of an occasionally brilliant, insecure, domineering personality incapable of achieving the wholeness he sought. "But in the last analysis Jung's search for the Holy Grail of conjunction failed. His syntheses did not eventuate in genuine union; they were makeshift soldering jobs, contrived amalgamations, rather than transcendent integrations of the opposites."[20] Stern's work, by comparison to the apologetic studies, presents an entirely different portrait of Jung. Although it has a useful "demythologizing" effect, one must be aware of his generally negative attitude towards Jung's work. There are, in addition, other critical accounts of Jung's thought, which I will discuss in the following section.

Generally, then, what we have in Hannah's and Stern's assessments of Jung's quest for wholeness are accounts that seek either to defend or to attack his life and work. These approaches are, in part shaped by the ongoing Freud/Jung controversy in which Jung is viewed as either a "misguided Freudian," or as an innovator showing the "right way to wholeness." This is not to detract from their respective works; used together, they present a multifaceted perspective of Jung's life.[21]

There is, however, a major difference between these studies and the present one. This is not a biographical account of Jung's life, but a study of the religious goal of his psychotherapeutic system. Thus, my focus is on the ideal level of Jung's thought, not the real level of his day-to-day life. Instead of debating whether Jung *really did achieve wholeness*, I will concentrate on what he held as the *ideal of human attainment*. Although both levels of investigation are valid, they are clearly of a different order.

Religious Studies

Scholars have employed a variety of methods in their attempts to approach Jung's thought from a religious perspective. Some theologians, for instance, view Jung's work as enhancing Christian theory and praxis. This is best illustrated in Morton Kelsey's *Christo Psychology*, where Kelsey utilizes Jung's writings for developing a "Christian psychology."

> While expressing our great debt and gratitude for Jung's contributions to our self-understanding and our religious world view, we will try not to overlook Jung's shortcomings. What we are trying to provide is a Christian psychology, based on the deepest understanding of Jesus Christ and utilizing the carefully developed findings of depth psychology.[22]

Similarly, the works of John Dourley and Wallace Clift seek to reconsider basic Christian doctrine in light of the findings of analytical psychology.[23] In these works, select aspects of Jung's thought, such as his writings on individuation, are used to revitalize and reinterpret the Christian message. Still other Christian writers view Jung's work as a threat to Christian doctrine;

their response is to defend the Christian position in the face of this perceived threat. Such writers fear that, as a result of Jung's psychological analysis of religion, God's transcendence will be reduced, as one scholar put it, to a "Jungian archetype at best."[24] But despite substantial differences between the hostile and friendly positions, there is the commonality of viewing Christian doctrine from a normative Jungian perspective. The main intention of these studies, then, is either to refute or to appropriate Jung's thought as part of a larger theological enterprise.

On the other hand, some studies attempt to show the influence of religious factors on Jung's work or to compare his thought to other religious systems. Good examples of the former are found in Harold Coward's *Jung and Eastern Thought*.[25] Here, in such articles as "Jung's Encounter with Yoga" and "The Influence of Yoga on Jungian Psychology," the effect of Eastern thought on the development of Jung's ideas is examined.[26] Comparative studies of Jung's work are also found in Coward's book as well as in Nathan Katz's edited work, *Buddhist and Western Psychology*. These studies usually compare selected aspects of Jung's system with basic concepts of Eastern traditions, as for example Katz does in his essay "On the Phenomena of the 'Feminine' according to Tantric Hagiographical Texts and Jungian Psychology."[27] On the Christian side, Jung's theories have been compared with the thought of everyone from St. Paul to Paul Tillich.[28] In general, then, the aim of the above studies is to elucidate the relationship between Jung's system and other traditions, or to show the various religious influences on the development of his ideas.

Another type of religious approach, represented by such scholars as Gerald May and Philip Rieff, seeks to evaluate the adequacy of Jung's thought as a religious ideology. In their view, Jung's system is deficient as an ideology when compared to "traditional" religious systems. Specifically, they see his thought as "nonreligious" or "quasi-religious" at best. In Rieff's words: "This is religion of a sort—for spiritual dilettantes, who collect symbols and meanings as others collect paintings. . . . But his doctrine is not the stuff of which religious systems are made: his lifework was a failure."[29]

May goes even further by claiming that there is nothing

religious about Jung's system:

> Much as we might like to believe that Jung's process of indi-
> viduation ... means to grow in realization of one's spiritual
> reality, and much as we might like to believe that "self-
> realization" or even "mental health" are synonymous with
> spiritual awakening, we cannot hold to such beliefs for long
> without closing or at least narrowing the Question. ... As I
> have said before, psychology simply is not big enough to
> incorporate human spiritual longing.[30]

Here May clearly indicates that Jung's system is incapable of
producing "real" spiritual growth, a conclusion he reaches by
comparing Jung's thought to what May considers "authentic"
religion.[31] He does this by first assuming the existence of a "core
identity of religion," which he describes as "mysterious, spiritual and willing."[32] He then proceeds to contrast Jung's system
with this "core identity," from which he concludes that Jung's
work is not an "authentic" form of religion. On this basis, he
concurs with Rieff that Jung's thought is an inadequate replacement for "traditional" religious ideologies.

A final religious study worthy of mention is James Heisig's
important work *Imago Dei*, in which Heisig examines Jung's
writings on religious phenomena, particularly the evolution of
Jung's concept of the "god image."[33] In this book, Heisig makes
a detailed analysis of Jung's interpretation of religious experience, showing the development of his views about religion.
Basically, his study is concerned with an examination of Jung's
psychological understanding of religion, such as is found in
Jung's well-known work *Psychology and Religion*.[34]

In summary, the broad range of religious studies include:
appraising the validity of Jung's system as a religious ideology;
studying his interpretation of religious experience; comparing
his thought to various religious thinkers; or appropriating his
thought for theological purposes. By contrast, I will examine
the religious goal of Jung's psychotherapeutic system. This
endeavor is quite different from the focus of those studies
mentioned above; as valid as those works are, they are not
concerned specifically with an analysis of the ultimate concern
of Jung's theoretical writings.

Historical Studies

These studies bear directly on my research, since a major concern of the historian of religions is to trace the evolution of a thinker's religious goal. Unfortunately, though, there are very few historical studies of Jung's thought, and those that are available are of a general nature. Lewis, for example, is concerned with Jung's early years, beginning with his doctoral dissertation *On the Psychology of So-called Occult Phenomena* (1902) and ending with his *Two Essays on Analytical Psychology* (1928).[35] Similarly, Lambert focuses on some of the major themes in Jung's later writings, while Aniela Jaffe's essay "The Creative Phases in Jung's Life" presents an overview of Jung's work in its entirety.[36] None of these scholars, however, address themselves to any one aspect of Jung's thought in particular; rather they attempt a developmental survey of his work in general. Although helpful, these studies are only the first step in clarifying the evolution of the religious goal of Jung's thought.

Individuation Studies

Since I maintain that the stages of Jung's religious goal (the quest for wholeness) are formulated in the individuation process, I now turn to those secondary sources concerned specifically with that process. Despite numerous studies of the individuation process, none have attempted a complete historical survey ranging over Jung's *Collected Works*. Previous studies can be arranged in three categories. Works in the first category attempt a general overview of Jung's thought, covering major theoretical components of his system, without, however, tracing the formation of those components. The works by Hall, Storr, and Whitmont are good illustrations of this approach.[37]

Jolande Jacobi's classic work on individuation takes a similar approach.[38] Moving freely through the *Collected Works*, she synthesizes Jung's writings on individuation into a single process. Here again, no effort is made to preserve chronology; instead one is left with the impression that Jung made one statement about individuation and that no later elaboration took place. The works of Edward Edinger and Josef Goldbrunner also fall into this ahistorical category in that they too combine Jung's varied writings on individuation into a single process.[39] All these studies result in a reification of that which was evolving throughout Jung's life.

There are, in addition to the ahistorical approach, historical studies of the individuation process. Henri Ellenberger takes as his point of departure for understanding Jung's thought the so-called "critical years" (1914-1919).[40] According to Ellenberger, the main components of the individuation process grew out of Jung's confrontation with the unconscious. Generally speaking this is correct, but somewhat misleading since this view fails to acknowledge later developments of the individuation process. Admittedly Jung formulated the key components of individuation during the critical years, although this is by no means the only formulation that he gave. Despite a superlative job of tracing the evolution of Jung's thought in general, Ellenberger too ends up treating the individuation process in an ahistorical manner.

Peter Homans takes a position closely aligned to Ellenberger's in that he also focuses on the critical years.[41] But for Homans, the key for explaining those years is found in Heinz Kohut's writings on narcissism. In Homans' view, Jung had formed a narcissistic relationship with Freud, the dissolution of which threw him into an intense crisis experience. The "core elements" (individuation process) thus resulted from Jung's attempt to sever his symbiotic relationship with Freud and to establish an independent identity.

My central concern with Homans' analysis is his claim that the "core elements" of the individuation process were established once and for all during the critical years. "I argue . . . that the leading original ideas that make up Jung's psychology were consolidated at the end of this critical period; that they were intimately related to Jung's personal experience at that time . . . and that they underwent little significant change thereafter."[42] I agree with the first two points but take exception with the last—that "little significant change" occurred in the "core element" after the critical years. Homans' claim is based on Jung's works from the first half of his life, most notably the *Two Essays on Analytical Psychology*. With respect to the individuation process (core process), Homans argues that "the essence of the core process lies in these last two works."[43] What Homans fails to notice, however, is that the version of the individuation process presented in the *Two Essays* is quite different from the one found in Jung's later alchemical writings.[44] References to those writings where Jung elaborates his initial understanding of individuation are, except for one passing reference, totally missing. This is a major omission when one considers that Jung spent nearly thirty years researching alchemy; three entire volumes of the *Collected Works* are committed to this topic.[45]

It is, therefore, somewhat misleading to speak of individuation as if Jung, once having formulated his thought, never elaborated upon it. So, whereas the ahistorical approach synthesizes Jung's early and late writings into a unified whole, Homans' approach takes the early formulation of individuation as paradigmatic. The problem with both approaches is that they fail to account for change and development.

Two recent studies have attempted to move away from the reification of the individuation process. Mattoon, in her book *Jungian Psychology in Perspective*, describes three ways of viewing individuation: ". . . as the development of the attitudes and function, making archetypal contents conscious, and [as] an alchemical process."[46] Although a step beyond the previous two approaches, it is nonetheless deficient as a historical study, since no attempt is made to follow the evolution of the individuation process throughout Jung's life. Likewise, James Hillman, in his insightful article "The Great Mother, Her Son, Her Hero, and the Puer," acknowledges the different formulations of the individuation process.[47] Hillman compares individuation in Jung's early writings (*Symbols of Transformation*) with his later alchemical works (*Mysterium Coniunctionis*).[48] Despite the considerable merits of this study, an examination of crucial texts is still missing. A major omission, to name but one, is the absence of the *Two Essays on Analytical Psychology*, which provides still yet another version of the individuation process.

The review of the literature is now complete. As we have seen, none of the biographical, religious, or historical studies are concerned with an investigation of the religious goal of Jung's system. Although the works on individuation do examine the self and its realization, they do not undertake a complete historical survey of that process. So, by contrast to these works, this study will both identify and document the religious goal found in Jung's theoretical writings. It is hoped that along with these other approaches, the religio-historical method, by furnishing an additional perspective from which to view Jung's thought, will provide insight into the development, formation, and elaboration of the religious goal of Jung's psychotherapeutic system.

RELIGIO-HISTORICAL METHOD

My study of Jung's thought is based on the religio-historical method proposed by Robert Baird in his book *Category Formation and the History of Religions*.[49] In that work, Baird indicates a number of crucial decisions confronting the historian of religions in the course of his/her investigations, chief among which is the scholar's understanding and use of definition. Baird, following Richard Robinson's work on definition, describes various types of definitions and their implications for the historian of religions.[50]

According to Robinson, there are two main classes of definitions—nominal and real. Robinson further divides nominal definition into word-word and word-thing definitions. As a subcategory under word-thing definition he includes lexical and stipulative definitions.[51] For our purposes, we need only concern ourselves with the differences between stipulative and real definitions, since it is this distinction which serves as the basis for Professor Baird's religio-historical method.

Real definitions, according to Robinson, are used to define things or, more exactly, to define the essence of things. The roots of this type of definition are found in the works of Socrates, Plato, and Aristotle. As Robinson points out, these thinkers were attempting to respond to the question, What is X? That is to say, they were not attempting to define the use of a word but rather the essence of a thing, such as piety or knowledge.[52] In addition to the search for essences, real definitions are often used in an attempt to discover "some identity in all the applications of an ambiguous word."[53] This approach, however, usually leads to confusion, since ambiguous words, by definition, have more than one lexical meaning. The insistence on one "true" meaning does not remove the ambiguity—only a stipulative definition can do that.

There are two further characteristics of real definitions: they are either true or false, and they usually come at the end of one's study. Because the aim of a real definition is to give a true account of an object, it ordinarily appears at the end of one's study, after a thorough analysis of the object.[54] The main point, then, to keep in mind when dealing with real definitions is that they are not about words, but about things. Whether in the form of a search for essences, the attempt to find the identity of a variety of word usages, or the analysis of an object, real definitions seek to make a true statement about the object itself.

Whereas a real definition is used to define things, a stipulative definition is used to define words or as Robinson puts it, to "report or establish the meaning of a symbol."[55] Thus a stipulative definition is the correlation of a certain word with a specified object, not a true description of an object. This implies that a stipulative definition is arbitrary—that is, one "self-consciously" proposes to assign a certain meaning to a word. But at the same time, as Robinson warns, one should "aim at preserving as much as possible of the intention and ideal implicit in the ordinary use of the word."[56]

The main advantage of stipulating the use of a word is the removal of ambiguity, which ensures "that we are all talking about the same thing when we use the same word."[57] Furthermore, stipulative definitions, by contrast to real definitions, usually appear at the beginning of one's study (since it is a proposal about word usage), not at the end as the result of one's investigation. Because stipulative definitions are always about words, they are neither true nor false, but either useful or not.[58] Their usefulness lies in the removal of ambiguity, which allows the scholar to proceed with his/her investigation. We now turn to the implications of definition for the historian of religions.

The historian of religions must decide whether to proceed with a stipulative or real definition of religion. Those scholars who opt for the latter type proceed by means of what Baird has called the essential-intuitional method.[59] That is to say, they do not begin their work with a definition of "religion" but assume that everyone knows what the word means. This approach pre-supposes, as Baird has pointed out, that religion "corresponds to something that has univocal ontological status . . . and that the reality or essence which it names is intuitively identifiable."[60] Accordingly, the scholar's definition of "religion" is not a pro-posal about the use of a word but an assertion about the true nature of the thing religion.

If, however, the historian of religions employs a stipulative definition, then he/she will begin by indicating how the word "religion" will be used throughout the study. Since "religion" is a lexically ambiguous term, a stipulative definition provides a single meaning for the use of the word. We are not concerned with the truth or falsity of our definition because we are not defining the essential qualities of the thing religion. Instead we are simply stipulating word usage. As Richard Comstock has clearly indicated, "the word 'religion' as now used by scholars has the stipulated meaning they have assigned to it, not one determined by some religious quality inherently present in the data to which the word is supposed to refer."[61]

For the purposes of this study, then, I define religion as "ultimate concern."[62] This definition, however, should not be confused with the one given by Paul Tillich in which an infinite, unconditional form of ultimacy is the object of one's concern. For Tillich, his definition serves as the point of departure for making normative judgements about true and false types of ultimate concerns.[63] My use of ultimate concern, on the other hand, does not involve a normative evaluation of the object of one's concern; rather by ultimate I am simply referring to a "concern which is more important than anything else for the person or community involved."[64] From an essentialist perspec-tive one may argue that such a definition of religion is simply too inclusive and does not do justice to the true essence (how-ever envisioned) of religion. But, again, as Comstock has argued: "These objections are valid only so long as it is assumed that a definition of religion must designate an essence. However, if it is agreed that such an approach to definition must be abandoned, then this particular critique . . . is no longer viable."[65]

More precisely, an ultimate concern, then, is a belief or value which is not defended by an appeal to a higher authority but is awarded the status of a fundamental, self-evident truth by the person holding it.[66] Consequently, my investigation centers on the human formulation of ultimacy—whatever form that takes—not on the validity of the concern itself. As an historian, my aim is to "describe the human past accurately, not to pronounce about it."[67] Thus, in the context of this study, I will not be making normative judgements about the ontological status of Jung's religious goal, nor will I attempt to criticize or defend Jung's work; rather, I will attempt to describe his thought in as objective a manner as possible.

Note, however, that I am not claiming that "ultimate concern" is the only or true definition of religion; rather, I am proposing a stipulative definition of religion, not a real one. Instead of assuming that certain things are inherently religious, this method takes the position that "there are only data of which we ask the religious question. Those data can include temples, beliefs, rites, defense systems, economic systems, artistic representations, political movements, etc."[68] In theory, then, the religio-historical question can be asked of any body of data, including psychological systems. Although using somewhat different language, the historian of religions Mircea Eliade makes a similar point:

> We must get used to the idea of recognizing hierophanies absolutely everywhere, in every area of psychological, economic, spiritual and social life. Indeed, we cannot be sure that there is anything—object, movement, psychological function, being or even game—that has not at some time in human history been somewhere transformed into a hierophany. . . . [69]

Viewed in that light, my claim that the quest for wholeness functions as the religious goal of Jung's psychotherapeutic system should not seem misplaced; it will only appear so if one insists on taking an essentialist view of religion.

Furthermore, it must be decided whether to investigate Jung's ultimate concern on the ideal (theoretical) or real (biographical) level.[70] In this study I will focus on the ideal level—that is, on what Jung believed should be of ultimate importance even though this ideal may not have been in accord with the reality of his day-to-day life. This is an important distinction, since I am claiming that it was not until the second or formative period that Jung consolidated his ultimate concern. During the first or developmental phase, there is no evidence in his theoretical writings that he had as yet consolidated his ultimate concern. Indeed, it was not until the formative period, after his crisis experience, that he first proposed the attainment of wholeness as the religious goal of his system. This is not to say, however, that Jung may not have had a religious goal on the real level prior to the second period; but that is not the concern of this study. Rather, my aim is to trace the development, formation, and elaboration of what Jung considered the ideal or ultimate goal of human existence.

We must, moreover, be sensitive to the many variations that an ultimate concern may take. "The same category of ultimacy with different auxiliary beliefs, a partial pattern being emphasized at a given period, new questions and new answers being formulated in an emerging truth system, the same beliefs as in another period but reordered and revalued in such a way as to appear new, and so forth."[71] In Jung's case we must distinguish between his ultimate concern and his formulation of a pattern of ultimacy. A pattern of ultimacy "is the complex of beliefs as related to the subject's primary notion of ultimacy which was held for a demonstrable period of time."[72] According to Jung's use of the term, individuation designates both a process and a goal. As a goal it refers to the realization of the self (*Selbstverwirklichung*), while as a process it refers to the stages or "way" leading to that goal (*der Weg der Individuation*).[73] Specifically, then, my thesis is that both Jung's ultimate concern and pattern of ultimacy underwent elaboration during the last period of his life. Although the ultimate concern of his system during the third phase remained the quest for wholeness, the way in which this was understood and the way to achieve it was further elaborated as part of Jung's "emerging truth system."

Finally, in order to validate my claims, I must briefly address the issue of religio-historical understanding. Professor Baird has stipulated a definition of understanding as "any valid knowledge about religion communicable in propositional form.[74] Accordingly, religio-historical understanding occurs when we have "descriptively true statements" about Jung's ultimate concern, which can be validated by the available historical data. I am, of course, assuming here that Jung's system has a religious goal. However, rather than arbitrarily imposing this conclusion *a priori* onto the data, I am simply suggesting that this claim can be verified by an examination of the data. Only after having evaluated all the evidence will we be able to determine whether this hypothesis is warranted.

TEXTUAL CONSIDERATIONS

One encounters a number of difficulties in attempting a historical study of Jung's thought. First, the *Collected Works* are edited according to themes, irrespective of chronology. Hence volume three, for example, contains articles ranging in time from 1907 to 1958.[75] Second, Jung himself complicated matters by revising earlier writings in light of latter developments in his thought; instead of allowing earlier ideas to stand, the revisions tend to blur the evolution of his thought. And finally, the archetypal, ahistorical nature of his thought does not readily lend itself to historical study. Indeed, one may even argue that a historical approach to Jung's thought may result in a distortion of his writings. But in a letter to Jolande Jacobi dated 24 September 1948 Jung wrote: "The systematic elaboration of my ideas, which were often just thrown out, is a task for those who come after me. . . ."[76] I take this to mean that a study aimed at clarifying the evolution of Jung's ideas does not constitute an unjustifiable imposition or distortion.

A further textual issue concerns the types of documentation used in this study.[77] Primary contemporaneous documentation refers to material written by Jung at the time when he held a particular belief. Jung's *Collected Works*, his letters, and earlier editions of works later revised, all fall within this category. In particular, the twenty-volume *Collected Works* will serve as the primary source of data for this study, and will include (where appropriate) the use of first editions of works later revised. Since Jung was continually revising earlier writings, recourse to first editions will better allow us to trace the evolution of his thought. I will, of course, clearly indicate references from earlier editions. The letters of Jung, especially those to Freud, will serve mainly to fill in biographical information during the early years. I might also add that there are other sources of primary contemporaneous documentation that I will not use. Most notably this includes over fifty additional volumes of unedited seminar transcripts, which are to be published as a series parallel to the *Collected Works*.[78]

Secondary contemporaneous documentation are those statements written by someone other than Jung at the time they were held by Jung and include reports of conversations by those who knew Jung personally. Like the letters, I will use this source primarily for biographical information. Primary later documentation are those statements made by Jung in retrospect, that is, statements he made after a particular belief was held. His autobiography, which is the chief example of this type of documentation, will be used to corroborate primary contemporaneous documentation (most notably the *Collected Works*), and to provide additional biographical information. As is well known, this work contains a mixture of historical fact and later psychological interpretations of his life experiences. Thus, I have relied on this work mostly for its chronology of events rather than for its interpretive significance.

And finally, secondary later documentation refers to accounts of beliefs made by others subsequent to the time they were held by Jung. Biographies and interpretive secondary studies are representative of this type of literature. Since these studies have already been referred to in the literature review, they will not be incorporated into the main part of the study, except where it is absolutely necessary to do so.

Part II

Developmental Phase (1895–1913)

Chapter Two

Psychic Fragmentation

The developmental phase represents the time prior to the formulation of Jung's ultimate concern, beginning with his university years and ending with his separation from Sigmund Freud. During this period Jung was concerned with establishing a professional identity and finding his place in the social order. His research interests centered on the scientific study of the human mind, and although his theoretical writings contain no evidence of a religious goal, a number of themes emerge which later influenced the formulation of his ultimate concern.

Specifically, the developmental phase of Jung's life can be divided into four subphases, consisting of his university studies, the development of his "complex" theory, his work on dementia praecox, and his involvement with the thought of Sigmund Freud. During each of these periods, Jung's research exhibits a variety of interests and concerns, but generally speaking, two preliminary observations can be made about his thought. His main concern was to explore the fragmented, neurotic, and at times psychotic, aspects of the human mind, which he did in a number of different ways and from a variety of perspectives. In addition, toward the end of this period, his writings show an interest in the process of psychic transformation. In order to preserve historical continuity, I will begin by examining these early interests, since they set the stage for much of Jung's later work.

UNIVERSITY STUDIES

In 1895, despite preparing to begin his university education, Jung's life was without focus or direction. He was not sure about anything—neither what he believed, nor what he wanted to study.[1] His concern was simply to acquire an education so that he could function in society; he realized that he had "to go forward—into study, moneymaking, responsibilities, entanglements, confusions, errors, submissions, defeats."[2] Hence he decided to enroll at Basel University and specialize in the study of medicine.

Despite the demands of family and studies, Jung found time to become a member of the Zofingia, a Swiss student society, where he participated in a number of discussions. In the latter part of his university years Jung's involvement in the Zofingia increased to the point where he was elected its president in 1897. These talks have recently been published and provide valuable insight into Jung's thinking at this time.[3] During the same period Jung was an observant at a number of seances. His observations and analysis of these seances formed the main body of his doctoral dissertation *On the Psychology and Pathology of So-called Occult Phenomena*.[4] Taken together, the two works from this period contain the stirrings of Jung's new-found interest in psychology.

Beginning with his Zofingia lectures, Jung prepared the ground for empirical and descriptive studies of various psychic phenomena. In the first of these lectures," The Border Zones of Exact Science" (given 28 November 1896), Jung's concerns are twofold: to criticize the limits of "materialistic sciences," and to argue for "a solid point of departure for further critical excursuses in the realm of metaphysics."[5] Most of the lecture, however, is taken up with the former issue, which is clearly stated in the beginning of his talk. "Although I know it is a waste of energy for me to combat materialism, nevertheless I hope to draw a clearer portrait of this absurd colossus with feet of clay . . . To this end, in the present study I attempt to supply a critical description of the theories and hypothesis of the exact sciences."[6] It is not until the end of the lecture that Jung argues for a widening of the domain of scientific investigation, although no specific research proposals are given.

In his second talk, "Some Thoughts on Psychology," Jung postulates a "life force" (the soul) existing independent of time and space. Although not a physical phenomenon as such, it is, according to Jung, still worthy of scientific investigation. He strongly suggests that "people ought to engage in experimental research into psychic phenomena," including such occurences as hypnotism and telepathy.[7] Jung's fourth lecture, given in the summer of 1898, develops further the general ideas of the first two and is noteworthy for the questions he raises about the nature and purpose of human existence. In an attempt to address the issue of human happiness, he posits a dualism between material success and inner development. "The assumption that happiness lies in external factors is for the most part an a priori judgement, i.e., most people do not have the slightest inkling that happiness could consist in anything else."[8] Jung, on the other hand, argues that happiness can be found in the "unfathomable depths of our own being," a theme that was to play an increasingly important role in his later writings.[9] But while clearly favoring an inner basis for happiness, Jung does not indicate any specific agenda at this time. Instead, it is best to view these talks as exploratory rather than definitive in nature.

With the encouragement of his adviser, Dr. Eugen Bleuler, Jung attempted to explore further some of his lecture themes in his doctoral dissertation *On the Psychology and Pathology of So-called Occult Phenomena*. Since Jung had been arguing for an expansion of scientific research into metaphysical domains, he viewed his study of a medium as a purely scientific undertaking. His research began in 1899 when he attended a number of seances held by a fifteen-year old woman named Helene Preiswerk, a second cousin of Jung's on his mother's side. Jung describes what he observed as the spirit began to take over the medium: She "grew very pale, slowly sank to the ground or into a chair, closed her eyes, became cataleptic, drew several deep breaths, and began to speak."[10] Jung observes, moreover, that it was like two personalities existing in one person: her normal waking state and her mediumistic trance state. In his analysis of the case Jung detected the presence of a further split within the mediumistic state itself and suggested that these fragmented psychic elements possess a certain autonomy of their own. This observation, which led him to infer the existence of independent, subconscious contents, was a preliminary formulation of his theory of the complex.[11]

In addition to the fragmentation of the psyche, Jung postulated the presence of a deeper underlying unity in the personality that struggles to overcome the dissociation. This dialectical relationship between fragmentation and unity was to become a central component in Jung's later works on individuation. At this time, however, his ideas concerning psychic unity are not fully developed but exist in the form of an "explanatory hypothesis," stating that the fragmentation of the personality does not reach into "the firmly knit basis of the ego-complex."[12] He further hypothesizes that perhaps the split-off aspects of the personality are really "future personalities" which, due to various "unfavorable circumstances," end up disrupting consciousness.[13]

In summarizing Jung's work during his university years a number of themes emerge. First, he has taken a descriptive approach to the study of the psyche, viewing it as an object of scientific study. And while it is true that he was studying subjective events, he was not engaged in a systematic exploration of his own psychic contents, at least to the extent that he would be during his crisis years. Moreover, we must remember that the term *psyche* refers to both a conscious and subconscious level; Jung did not make any further distinctions in the structure of the mind at this time. Instead most of his attention is directed to the fragmented nature of the subconscious mind and its effect on consciousness. Although all these ideas are still in embryonic form, it is nonetheless clear that a certain direction has taken shape in Jung's research. He was now ready to begin his study of the human psyche in earnest.

THE "COMPLEX" THEORY

Jung arrived at Burghölzli Psychiatric Hospital December 1900, where he worked as Dr. Eugen Bleuler's first assistant. Jung leaves little doubt that while at Burghölzli his dominant research interest was the exploration of the pathological aspects of the human mind. "Dominating my interest and research was the question: What actually takes place inside the mentally ill?"[14] From this, it is clear that Jung still viewed the psyche as a source of data to be studied, not as the basis of an ultimate concern; he was simply interested in the diagnosis and cure of various mental disorders.

His most important discovery during this period was the idea of the "complex", which he defined as an unconscious psychic fragment that causes various mental disturbances. In a 1904 publication "On Hysterical Misreading" Jung applies his theory of psychic fragmentation to a case of hysterical misreading, from which he concludes that the act of replacing one word for another while reading a text indicates the presence of autonomous psychic elements.[15] "The reason why I attach particular importance to hysterical misreading is that it demonstrates in a nutshell the splitting off of psychic functions from the ego-complex, which is such a characteristic of hysteria, and consequently the strong tendency of the psychic elements towards autonomy."[16] It was precisely this interest in the fragmentation of the psyche that led Jung to begin his work on the word association test as a means to verify his "complex" theory.

As early as 1903 Jung published a case analysis using the word association test, but it was not until 1904, with the publication of "The Associations of Normal Subjects," that we receive a detailed work devoted solely to the association experiment.[17] This work is significant for a number of reasons. First, it shows Jung working as an experimental psychologist—in the tradition of such pioneers as Galton and Wundt—to provide an empirical base for his previous theory of psychic fragmentation. It is also important because Jung felt that this work furnished scientific proof for Freud's theories of repression and the unconscious.

Jung begins by specifying his goals: to collect and analyze the associations of normal subjects, and to establish a basis for comparing and evaluating mentally disturbed cases.[18] Thirty-eight subjects from a variety of socioeconomic backgrounds were involved. The test method was to present the subject with a stimulus word, and to record the response and reaction-time. Four hundred stimulus words were used in the experiment, and an elaborate interpretive system was designed to analyze faulty associations. Such things as failures to respond, extended reaction-times, repetitions of the stimulus word, meaningless associations, and multi-word responses all indicated an underlying disturbance in the subject's association. The remaining associations were evaluated and statistically grouped together according to types of responses. For example, all associations based on rhymes formed a separate category.

Interspersed between the pages of statistical classifications, Jung uses his "complex" theory to explain the various faulty reactions he encounters.[19] He hypothesizes that a fragmented aspect of the psyche impinging on ego-consciousness is responsible for interrupting the association process. Since a complex is an emotionally charged sum of psychic energy that constellates various associations around it, Jung thought that whenever a stimulus word touched on a complex, attention was drawn away from consciousness to the complex, thereby causing the increased reaction time. "Practically every lengthening of reaction-time, even within quite normal limits . . . signifies, as far as we know at present, that the particular stimulus-word has touched upon a feeling-toned complex."[20] In short, Jung felt that any reaction of more than 5.0 seconds was a sure indication of a complex, and that an "overwhelming number of the complexes" were of an erotic nature, although certainly not all complexes were limited to sexual causes. The remainder of his publications during this period were revisions, explanations, and applications of his "complex" theory.

In 1905, for example, after analyzing the associations of epileptic patients in order to compare their associations with his findings on "normal" subjects, he concludes that despite some variation, the presence of an underlying complex is present in both groups, with only the nature of the complexes showing differences.[21] This study was followed by a refinement of the reaction-time ratio in the association test, in which Jung explains the extended delays in reactions by the existence of "a mass of images held together by a particular affect" (the feeling-toned complex).[22] These studies strengthened Jung's belief that the unconscious and its complexes were the source of disturbances in consciousness. In a 1905 article on cryptomnesia he makes the following statement:

> We must always bear in mind that conscious psychic phenom-
> ena are only a very small part of our total psyche. By far the
> greater part of the psychic elements in us is unconscious . . .
> Our unconscious must therefore harbour an immense number
> of psychic complexes which would astonish us by their
> strangeness.[23]

In this quote Jung implicitly couples his theory of the complex
with the idea of the unconscious, while in another article he
writes that our "ego-consciousness is merely the marionette that
dances on the stage, moved by a concealed mechanism."[24] By
this he means that ego-consciousness is not a sovereign agent,
but is subject to unconscious psychic forces beyond its control.
These psychic factors, due to their incompatible nature, have
been split off from consciousness, and now act in opposition to
it. This is a theory of personality based on fragmentation and
conflict, a view that pervades Jung's work throughout this period.

At this time Jung's work took a decisive turn in the direction of Freud's theories; indeed, a year later the correspondence
between them began. In a 1905 article on memory, a number of
key references are made to Freud.[25] Jung writes that a person's
inability to respond to some stimulus words is due to a repressed
complex, and that "the validity of this can be doubted only by
someone who has not himself tested Freudian psychoanalysis."[26]
By this time Jung was convinced that his association experiments were scientific proof of Freud's theories of repression,
neurosis, and the unconscious. His fascination with the "complex" theory and its relationship to psychoanalysis continued
to grow.

For example, in a 1906 paper "Psychoanalysis and the
Association Experiment" he proposes the use of the association
test as part of psychoanalytic treatment, believing that the test
can provide a quicker and more direct route to unearthing
repressed psychic contents.[27] He begins by extending his theory
into the realm of the "normal" personality, arguing that complexes are not limited to neurotic people; instead, "everybody
. . . has one or more complexes . . . "[28] This may seem like a
casual remark, but in fact, it is filled with significance, since
even the "normal" personality is now viewed as conflicted and

fragmented; the only difference between the "normal" and the "neurotic" person is that in extreme cases of mental illness the split-off psychic fragments overtake consciousness completely. Jung suggests that the goal of therapy is to bring these complexes to the surface of consciousness where they can then be disarmed. "The best energy-cure, however, is to force the patients, with a certain ruthlessness, to unearth and expose to the light the images that consciousness finds intolerable."[29] In other words, complexes are destroyed and neuroses ended, only when the complexes are released from the power of repression. Like Freud, Jung saw the lifting of repression as the key to overcoming neuroses.

Since Jung thought he had found the source of a variety of mental disturbances with his discovery of the complex, he turned his attention to the application of his theory to explain such mental disorders as dementia praecox and hysteria. In the case of hysteria, for instance, Jung felt that the patient suffers from "an old wound that still hurts," and one which the patient is unable to overcome.[30] And although all people have complexes, the complexes in hysterical patients are so emotionally charged that they overpower all other aspects of the personality. Thus the line between pathology and normality is only a matter of intensity. Jung also views the complex as playing an important role in dementia praecox, but his thoughts on this subject he reserved for his next major work, *The Psychology of Dementia Praecox*.[31]

THE PSYCHOLOGY OF DEMENTIA PRAECOX

Jung had become senior staff physician at the Burghölzli Hospital in Zurich by 1907 when he wrote his critically acclaimed monograph on dementia praecox. As Jung writes in the foreward, it is the "fruit of three years' experimental researches and clinical observations."[32] He also acknowledges his debt to Freud's theories although he openly admits differences with Freud, most notably the absolute importance that Freud attributes to sexuality; for Jung, even at this early date, Freud's theory is simply one among many possible explanations of mental illness. The basis for Jung's analysis of dementia is his previous work on the association experiment, particularly his idea of the complex.

This work starts with a thorough classification and analysis of previous theories of dementia praecox in which Jung credits, among others, Janet in pointing out the *abaissement du niveau mental* as characteristic of the dementia patient.[33] Jung contends that due to a "lowering of the mental level" the weakened ego is no longer able to prevent the complexes from entering consciousness. They then become a threat to conscious functioning, directly challenging the authority of the ego. Furthermore dementia exhibits a quality which Jung calls a "fixation of affects." Using a mixture of Freudian/Jungian language, he explains his position: "Fixation of affects therefore means, in Freudian terms, that the repressed complexes . . . can no longer be eliminated from the conscious process; they remain operative, and so prevent the further development of personality."[34]

But Jung takes his hypothesis for the origin of dementia a step further, speculating that whereas in hysteria the symptoms are reparable, with dementia the complex may have a physiological effect on the brain, perhaps producing a toxin that permanently injures the brain.[35] With this, Jung has positioned himself within a tradition of research on dementia; yet by proposing his theory of the complex, he has broken new ground. He now proceeds to explain his theory in full.

Despite claiming that the personality is composed of a variety of complexes, Jung makes no effort to explain how these diverse psychic units are held together, other than mentioning that the ego-complex is the most stable of all the complexes.[36] Cases of double personality are, for example, nothing other than an autonomous complex overpowering ego-consciousness; it is as if each complex is a personality unto itself, "distinguished by peculiarities of mood and character."[37] In extreme cases of neurosis, these complexes are easily activated due to their highly sensitive nature. The cause of these complexes are emotionally charged events that create deep-seated psychic wounds in the unconscious, around which ideas and associations, related to the trauma, constellate. Whenever a subsequent event occurs that touches on the repressed wound, an outburst of emotion results, thereby diverting psychic energy from the ego to the complex and preventing proper adaptation and response to immediate environmental stimuli. And if one of the secondary personalities succeeds in permanently replacing the ego, we then have a case of dementia praecox.

Also characteristic of dementia praecox is an "unruliness of affects" that disrupts the ego structure, causing a conflict between the complex and consciousness. With the weakening of the synthesizing power of the ego, the unconscious has free run of the psyche so that, cognitively, there is an inability to concentrate as attention is turned away from the external environment to the inner world of the complex. And when the autonomous complexes finally penetrate consciousness, they bring with them a multitude of distorted images. If the inner psychic images are then projected outward, hallucinations and delusions occur distorting the person's perception of reality, a condition Jung likens to a state of dreaming while awake.[38]

Therapeutically, Jung used dream analysis and the association test in his work with patients. Contrary to the accepted psychiatric practice of the day, he took his patients' fantasies seriously, and tried to understand the hidden meaning in them.[39] He found that by entering into the patient's world, he could get at the underlying "germ of meaning" in the fantasies, which in some cases helped produce a cure.[40] In essence he treated the hallucinations as he would a dream, asking the patient to free associate to the images. Like dreams, he thought that the symptoms symbolically expressed the "hopes and disappointments" of the patient's life.[41]

In summary, then, these years were a transitional period in Jung's life during which he began to build a professional identity, albeit one influenced by the work of others; but it was also a time during which he developed some theories of his own. We can therefore say that Jung's thought was still in development, heavily influenced by the work of others, yet showing signs of originality. With the conclusion of this period, Jung was ready to begin his much-heralded involvement with Sigmund Freud.

Chapter Three

Psychoanalytic Influence

Jung's involvement with Freud's ideas dates back to 1900 when he first read Freud's *The Interpretation of Dreams*, and to 1901 when he wrote a short summary of Freud's dream theory.[1] Likewise his dissertation and subsequent writings continued to make reference to Freud's work. Moreover, an examination of *The Freud/Jung Letters* reveals that Jung's research interests were heavily influenced by the psychoanalytic movement.[2] As Homans succinctly puts it: "During this time Jung's intellectual efforts shifted entirely, moving from his synthesis of descriptive psychiatry, experimental research, to a comprehensively Freudian orientation."[3] As for the actual relationship between the two men, it began in 1906 when Jung sent Freud a copy of *Diagnostic Association Studies*.[4] Freud's reply dated 11 April 1906 thanked Jung for the book, which Freud had previously purchased.[5] Freud then sent Jung a collection of short papers on the theory of neurosis, and Jung's response on 5 October 1906 began a correspondence that ran until April 1914.[6] Their correspondence is a valuable resource for tracing the further development of Jung's thought, and for determining the extent of Freud's influence on Jung.

In a 26 November 1906 letter Jung tells Freud how he "championed your [Freud's] causes" and moved Professor Gaupp "a little closer to our side. ... "[7] This quote refers to Jung's participation at a Congress of South-West German psychiatrists in Tübingen and helps to illustrate Jung's close association with Freud. That Jung's commitment to Freud was strong is further indicated by the following letter (#7): "Personally I am enthusiastic about your therapy and well able to appreciate its signal merits."[8] Similarly, in letter #9, Jung writes of "championing your standpoint," a phrase occurring numerous times throughout Jung's letters.[9]

This is not to say that Jung accepted Freud's theories in toto. We note a letter by Freud (#11) in which he accuses Jung of downplaying the role of sexuality.[10] But despite varying points of disagreement, the overall orientation of Jung's letters show a close identification with Freud's ideas. With respect to Freud's dream theory, for instance, Jung writes that he "is no longer plagued by doubts as to the rightness of your theory."[11]

On a personal level Jung's relationship with Freud went beyond a mere acceptance of Freud's ideas. In response to a previous letter from Freud (#38), Jung writes:

> But this I must say . . . : it is my honest enthusiasm for the truth that impels me to find some way of presenting your teachings that would best bring about a breakthrough. Otherwise my unconditional devotion to the defence and propagation of your ideas, as well as my equally unconditional veneration of your personality, would be bound to appear in an extremely peculiar light. . . .[12]

Phrases like "unconditional veneration of your personality" and "unconditional devotion to the defence and propagation of your ideas" suggest that Jung was heavily involved in psychoanalysis on a personal as well as theoretical level. Jung's veneration was to grow, so much so that in October 1907 Jung writes: "So the self-preservation complex does not come from there; it is rather that my veneration for you has something of the character of a 'religious crush.' "[13] Still later, he writes (#204) that "the basic principles of the psychoanalytic way of life have been observed pretty strictly. For my morning devotions I religiously analysed dreams."[14] These statements leave little doubt about the depth of Jung's personal involvement in the psychoanalytical movement.

On the theoretical level Jung's research (as might be expected) contains a strong pro-Freud emphasis. In a 1906 rebuttal to Aschaffenburg's criticism of psychoanalysis, Jung defends Freud's position on two points. The first concerns Aschaffenburg's attack on Freud's sexual theory. Despite falling short of claiming that all cases of hysteria have sexual roots, Jung is willing to admit that "an indefinitely large number of cases of hysteria derive from sexual roots."[15] The second part of Jung's rebuttal is addressed to Aschaffenburg's statement that psychoanalysis is nothing more than "suggestion." Here once again Jung counters by saying that no one can criticize the findings of psychoanalysis unless the methods have been personally used; in Aschaffenburg's case, according to Jung, this obviously has not been done.

In a 1908 article "The Freudian Theory of Hysteria" Jung returns to his theme of the fragmented psyche.[16] Using his "complex" theory, he holds with Freud that an early childhood trauma causes a repression of certain psychic contents that later impinge on consciousness. He then refers to his association studies as a means for detecting the underlying repressed complexes. Despite mild reservations about Freud's absolute claims, Jung maintains a more or less Freudian position. In short, we see during this period a gradual merging of Jung's idea of the complex with Freud's theories of repression and neurosis. This is clearly evident in Jung's review of Freud's dream theory where[17] he agrees with Freud's distinction of a manifest and latent dream content but adds that the dream is an expression of a hidden complex, which the dream censor disguises to prevent it from being recognized.[18] This is a prime example of a traditional Freudian notion being given a Jungian twist.

And as late as 1911 Jung's work was still showing signs of Freudian influence and continued psychoanalytic fervor. Nowhere is this better illustrated than in Jung's critical review of an article by Morton Prince.[19] In a previous publication, Prince had criticized the wish-fulfilling aspect of Freud's dream theory, and in his attempt to refute Prince, Jung reinterprets a number of dreams used by Prince in his criticism of Freud. Jung claims that Prince's error is in mistaking the manifest content for the latent content; but when analyzed according to this distinction, Freud's theory, in Jung's view, is upheld. Although Jung's writings from 1907-1911 place him squarely in the mainstream of the psychoanalytic movement, the seeds for the further development of his thought were beginning to take root.

BREAK WITH FREUD

Jung's growing dissatisfaction with Freud's ideas is particularly evident in the second half of *The Freud/Jung Letters* and in his autobiography where Jung mentions that the turning point in their relationship came on their trip to America in 1909.[20] While interpreting one of Freud's dreams, Jung requested further details from Freud, which he refused to give. Freud supposedly responded: "But I cannot risk my authority."[21] Jung tells how "that sentence burned into my memory; and in it the end of our relationship was already foreshadowed."[22] *The Letters* indicate, however, that Jung was still involved in the psychoanalytic movement, although he was no longer completely in the grip of Freud's ideas. Instead he was shifting his attention to the study of mythology.

In an October 1909 letter, Jung writes Freud of his new interest in mythology: "I am obsessed by the thought of one day writing a comprehensive account of this whole field, after years of fact-finding and preparation, of course. . . . Archaeology or rather mythology has got me in its grip. . . . "[23] Increasingly Jung's research interests were shifting to the study of mythology. In November 1909 he writes: "One of the reasons I didn't write for so long is that I was immersed every evening in the study of symbol. . . . "[24] These studies continued to move Jung further and further from Freud, which is evident in the following letter (#170). "I am turning over and over in my mind the problem of antiquity. . . . Without doubt there's a lot of infantile sexuality in it, but that is not all."[25] Here again, Jung is unable to accept Freud's sexual theory in its entirety.

I concur with Homans' view that Jung's preoccupation with mythology signals the initial stirrings of his involvement with his own fantasy life.[26] In his autobiography Jung points out the inadequacy of Freud's theories to interpret the symbolism of his dreams, which is one reason why Jung ventured into mythology—to understand his psychic contents at this time.[27] Jung correlates the relationship between symbolism and his psychic contents in a February 1910 letter: "All sorts of things are cooking in me, mythology in particular. . . . My dreams revel in symbols that speak volumes. . . ."[28]

We can thus characterize Jung's thought as still in development—this time, moving away from Freud toward an unknown future.

> I often feel I am wandering alone through a strange country, seeing wonderful things that no one has seen before and no one needs to see. It was like that when the psychology of Dementia praecox dawned upon me. Only, I don't yet know what will come of it. I must just let myself be carried along. . . .[29]

Professionally, too, Jung's life was showing signs of upheaval as Freud's August 1910 letter clearly indicates: "As it is, the first months of your reign, my dear son and successor, have not turned out brilliantly."[30] Jung's subsequent reply (#206) acknowledges this fact. "I realize that my debut has turned out less than brilliantly. . . ."[31] The tension between the two men is further echoed in a letter from Emma Jung to Freud, in which she too senses the growing estrangement between Freud and her husband.[32] Quite perceptively she points to Jung's new work in mythology as the source of the problem; and indeed, with the publication of the *Psychology of the Unconscious* the break between the two men was imminent.[33] The correspondence during this period is increasingly antagonistic, until finally on 8 June 1912 Jung writes Freud: "It seems I shall have to go my own way for some time to come."[34]

PSYCHOLOGY OF THE UNCONSCIOUS

This is the first English edition of *Symbols of Transformation* (revised 1952), later to become volume five of the *Collected Works*. My remarks refer to the original 1912 edition, which in style and content deviates from Jung's previous writings in a number of important ways.[35] Stylistically, it was written over a short period of time and was not a "polished" piece of writing like Jung's previous works. In retrospect Jung tells of his situation at the time. "It was written at top speed, amid the rush and press of my medical practice without regard to time or method. I had to fling my material together just as I found it. . . . The whole thing came upon me like a landslide that cannot be stopped."[36] The raw, rough quality of this work is evident throughout the nearly six hundred pages. Its content covers Freudian analysis, libido, incest, psychic transformation, mythology, and religion, of which three issues are most important for the development of Jung's ultimate concern: his reinterpretation of Freud's libido and incest theory; his reductionistic critique of religious beliefs; and his notion of psychic transformation.

The repudiation of Freud comes via a revision and expansion of the libido theory beyond its original sexual meaning to include psychic energy in general. In chapter two, "The Conception and the Genetic Theory of Libido," Jung summarizes Freud's original use of the term libido. "The chief source of the history of the analytic conception of libido is Freud's 'Three Contributions to the Sexual Theory'. There the term libido is conceived by him in the original narrow sense of sexual impulse, sexual need."[37] Jung then explains the need to widen this conception, particularly because he found it insufficient to describe the total loss of reality experienced by dementia patients. Instead of equating libido with sexual energy specifically, Jung equates libido with "psychic energy" in general; sexual energy is one of many possible manifestations of libido, but certainly not the only one.[38]

Consequently, he reinterpreted Freud's incest theory to mean a damming up and regression of libido to an earlier psychological stage of development. According to Jung, when viewed in this light, incest takes on a symbolic rather than literal meaning; instead of "cohabitation," the incest wish is the desire to retreat into the protective custody of the "mother" or unconscious matrix from which consciousness initially evolved.

But incest also symbolizes the desire for rebirth from the "mother," which requires a return of the libido to its unconscious source. Mythologically, Jung envisioned this as a descent of the hero into darkness.

> Whoever vanquishes this monster has gained a new or eternal youth. For this purpose one must, in spite of all dangers,

descend into the belly of the monster (journey to hell) and spend some time there (imprisonment by night in the sea). . . . The battle with the night serpent signifies, therefore, the conquering of the mother. . . .[39]

This descent is most crucial when a person is confronted with seemingly insurmountable life obstacles because, at such times, the libido is either permanently swallowed by the "mother" (the unconscious), or it finally succeeds in freeing itself from an earlier stage of development. The hero myth thus symbolizes the struggle of the person who has descended (regressed) to the primordial depths and succeeded in overcoming attachment to the "mother" (the unconscious). By so doing the hero is able to confront life's difficulties in an independent, direct manner. Put simply, whereas the reversal of the regressive flow of libido leads to adaptation to reality, consumption of the libido by the unconscious leads to a "willful prolonging of the infantile state" of childhood.[40]

Since a conflict exists between the forward striving of libido and its infantile regression, maturity requires a sacrifice of the latter. "Sacrifice means renouncing the mother, that is to say, renunciation of all bonds and limitations which the soul has taken with it from the period of childhood into the adult life."[41] The symbolism is obvious: rebirth of a new life requires the death of one's old, dependent self, or in Jung's words, "if he (the hero) is to live he must fight and sacrifice his longing for the past in order to rise to his own heights."[42] This implies that the birth of a larger, more mature sense of selfhood requires the overcoming of one's undeveloped, infantile self. This is Jung's version of a theory of adolescent development. "The childishness of character, which as yet is unable to understand that one must leave father and mother, . . . in order to serve the destiny of the entire personality."[43] Without explicitly mentioning the term *individuation*, the ideas of development, independence, and psychic wholeness are prototypical images later used by Jung. With this massive revisioning of Freud's theories, the relationship between the two men was, for all practical purposes, over.

While engaged in the process of revisioning Freud's theories, Jung was also busy reinterpreting religious symbolism in psychological terms. "Since, psychologically understood, the divinity is nothing else than a projected complex . . . , so God is to be considered as the representation of a certain sum of energy (libido)."[44] Here Jung is suggesting that religious images are actually psychological projections of psychic processes, a view that is in keeping with his previous position on mediumistic phenomena, where he interpreted the spirits as split-off parts (complexes) of the psyche. Accordingly, this means that the gods reside in the unconscious, although most believers, in Jung's view, are unaware of this situation.[45] He ultimately concludes that to worship the deity is tantamount to worshiping one's own "vital force, the libido" in projected form.[46]

As an alternative, Jung argues that through increased self-awareness we should confront our libido directly instead of doing so in its projected religious forms. "Man could without compulsion wish that which he must do, and this from knowledge, without delusions through belief in the religious symbols."[47] That is, in Jung's view, the replacing of belief by direct psychological knowledge would result in a reclamation of misplaced psychic energy; although religious beliefs are useful, they are an intermediary step which is now obsolete. Unfortunately, though, Jung had not yet constructed a comprehensive system of his own to fill the theoretical and religious void he had created. This would be the task of the formative years of his life.

His writings up through 1913 were further clarifications of the somewhat loosely organized views found in *Psychology of the Unconscious*. In 1912 Jung once again traveled to America, this time to give a series of nine lectures at Fordham University.[48] In those talks, he made a thorough presentation of Freud's theories as well as outlining his differences with Freud. Following his criticism of Freud in *Psychology of the Unconscious*, Jung gives his strongest condemnation of the libido theory. "I think there is nothing for it but to abandon the sexual definition of libido. . . ."[49] After proposing an expanded view of the libido as he did in *Psychology of the Unconscious*, he then reiterates his theory of the neurosis as a damming-up of libido that is forced to regress to an earlier stage of development when confronted with a seemingly insurmountable obstacle.[50] He speaks of his symbolic revisioning of the Oedipus complex and proposes a teleological rather than reductionistic view of dream interpretation. There is hardly anything new in these lectures; rather they stand, as I said, as clarifications of the material found in *Psychology of the Unconscious*.

One other article of importance was a 1913 publication on psychological typology, which was to serve as the basis for a major book on the subject.[51] This was Jung's first attempt to come to an understanding of the theoretical differences between Freud and Adler; but as Jung correctly observes, "the difficult task of creating a psychology which will be equally fair to both types must be reserved for the future."[52] It was not until the 1921 publication of *Psychological Types* that Jung fully addressed this issue.

SUMMARY OF THE DEVELOPMENTAL PHASE

Beginning with his Zofingia lectures, Jung prepared the ground for empirical and descriptive studies of various psychic phenomena. Specifically, in his doctoral dissertation Jung addressed the issue of occult phenomena from a psychological perspective, hypothesizing that mediumistic events were projections of splintered psychic contents. In his work with the association test, Jung then provided empirical evidence for these psychic fragments or feeling-toned complexes. His theory of the psyche at this time was based on fragmentation and conflict. He used his "complex" theory to explain the condition of dementia praecox as well as the structure of the "normal" personality; common to all persons in varying degrees was the presence of a multiplicity of psychic complexes. Fragmentation became the central feature of the human personality, and almost without fail, his writings during this period proclaimed the divided, conflicted nature of the psyche. Little attention, however, was given to overcoming these psychic splits.

Jung's use of psychoanalysis as a means to probe further the neurotic mind resulted in a blending of his "complex" theory with Freud's understanding of repression and neurosis. But as his interest turned to mythology, a gradual distancing from Freud occurred, until he finally began the process of revisioning aspects of Freud's theory. In addition to repudiating Freud, he also criticized religious beliefs as inadequate descriptions of human existence. The problem was, he had no replacement for either, leaving him with no orienting factor in his own life. This condition had a significant bearing on the subsequent formation of his ultimate concern, since by reducing external religious reality to projections of psychic energy Jung gave a heightened importance to inner psychic life; coupled with the significance he attributed to psychic transformation, it only remained for him to elevate this process to a position of ultimate importance. This was to coincide with his search during the formative phase of his life for a factor capable of unifying the fragmentation of the psyche.

Part III

Formative Phase (1913–1928)

Chapter Four

The Unconscious as
Locus of Ultimacy

During the formative phase Jung formulated his ultimate concern and pattern of ultimacy. Although still interested in the problem of psychic fragmentation, Jung's interest shifted to a search for a means to unify the psyche. Specifically, this search culminated in the formulation of the self as the unifier of the psyche and the individuation process as the way leading to that unity. Similarly, Jung's method of studying the psyche also shifted. No longer interested solely in the psyche as a source of data for scientific study, Jung engaged in a direct confrontation with his own psychic processes. Along with this confrontation came a gradual elevation of the process of psychic development to a level of ultimate importance. Instead of addressing penultimate therapeutic issues as he had in the previous period, Jung's claims about the self and its individuation took on a decidedly religious significance; that is, they were statements about the ultimate goal and purpose of human existence.

The main source of biographical documentation for this period is Jung's private journal the *Red Book*, which contains writings and drawings done by Jung during his confrontation with the unconscious. Although it was never published in its entirety, Aniela Jaffe, the editor of Jung's autobiography, had direct access to the contents of the *Red Book* and recently published a number of excerpts from it.[1] In addition, Jung gave an account of his experiences in his autobiography, which I have relied on for a general outline of his life during this period. Naturally, the theoretical part of my discussion relies on Jung's writings found in his *Collected Works*.

Whereas the previous phase in Jung's life was consumed by school, work, and family issues, this phase was devoted to the exploration of his own psychic processes. This shift in Jung's interests is expressed in a passage from the *Red Book*.

> By my fortieth year I had achieved everything I had wished for as a child. I had gained fame, power, wealth, knowledge, and the best human fortune. Then my desire for increasing these good things ceased, the desire retreated. . . . I felt the spirit of the depths, but I did not understand him.[2]

In response to "the spirit of the depths," Jung resigned as editor of the *Jahrbuch* in October 1913 and as president of the International Psychoanalytic Association in April 1914.[3] He was now completely on his own, no longer able to find support in his previous involvements with Freud. What then was Jung's ultimate concern at this time? Jung asked himself this very question: "But in what myth does man live nowadays? In the Christian myth, the answer might be, 'Do you live in it?' I asked myself. To be honest, the answer was no. For me, it is not what I live by. . . . 'But then what is your myth—the myth in which you do live?' "[4] Jung reports that he stopped thinking at this point because he felt uncomfortable with the direction this dialogue was taking.

The fact is, Jung was without an ultimate concern, something which was to cause him great confusion for the next six years. "A period of inner uncertainty began for me. It would be no exaggeration to call it a state of disorientation. I felt totally suspended in mid air. . . . "[5] He goes on to describe his feelings of panic, darkness, and tension, and how he resigned his administrative and teaching positions in order to devote himself fully to the exploration of the unconscious. In the following passage Jung tells of how his involvement with the unconscious filled his whole life. "For I felt that something great was happening to me, and I put my trust in the thing which I felt to be more important *sub specie aeternitatis*. I knew that it would fill my life, and for the sake of that goal I was ready to take any kind of risk."[6] Throughout this period, then, Jung struggled with his psychic processes in an attempt to come to a degree of self-understanding.

Jung's struggle can be viewed, among other things, as a religious crisis, in that he sought to construct a meaningful form of ultimacy for himself. Specifically, he went about this by shifting the focus of his life from outer, professional pursuits to an investigation of the inner world of the psyche. As Jung puts it: "Therefore my first obligation was to probe the depths of my own psyche. ... This work took precedence over everything else."[7] This marked a major shift in his attitude toward the psyche. Whereas previously he approached the psyche as an object of scientific investigation, he now viewed its exploration as an inner, personal necessity.

> I thought and spoke much about the soul; I knew many learned words about the soul; I judged it and made a scientific object of it.
>
> I did not consider that the soul cannot be the object of my judgment and knowledge. ...
>
> Therefore the spirit of the depths pressed me to speak to my soul, to call upon it as a living and independent being whose re-discovery means good fortune for me.[8]

Initially, however, he was at a loss of how to proceed in his psychic exploration. "But I knew no technique whereby I might get to the bottom of my inner processes, and so there remained nothing for me to do but wait, ... and pay close attention to my fantasies."[9] His fantasies, which had begun while he was working on the *Psychology of the Unconscious*, increased and consumed more and more of his attention. But despite attempts to give form to his inner life by constructing a miniature village from stone, his dreams and fantasies continued. Finally, though, he devised a means to establish contact with his fantasies by imagining a steep descent into the depths of his psyche. During his first attempt on 12 December 1913, he envisioned himself landing on a "soft, sticky mass" at the entrance to a dark cave where he encountered a corpse with a wound on his head, an image he later interpreted as a symbol of death and rebirth.[10] Then, six days later, he had a dream where he met the figure of Sigfried, from whom he learned that his "heroic idealism had to be abandoned, for there are higher things than the ego's will, and to these one must bow."[11]

In another psychic sojourn, Jung encountered a wise old man called "Elijah" and a young blind girl called "Salome," both of whom he approached and spoke to. In his autobiography Jung interpreted their presence as personifications of Logos and Eros.[12] In a related fantasy, Elijah turned into the figure of Philemon who, according to Jung, represented "superior insight." Philemon taught him that "there are things in the psyche which I do not produce, but which produce themselves and have their own life."[13] And finally, in still yet another fantasy, the figure of Ka appeared out of the earth, forming the "earthly" counterpart to the "spirited" Philemon figure.[14]

Since these figures were an important source of meaning and insight for Jung, he recorded them in the *Red Book* and carried on conversations with them. Jung's work with his fantasies indicates the increasing importance he attributed to the psyche: "I loved it and hated it, but it was my greatest wealth. My delivering myself over to it, as it were, was the only way by which I could endure my existence and live as fully as possible."[15] It is against this backdrop of psyche exploration that we now turn to an examination of Jung's theoretical writings. Such an investigation will permit us to view the initial steps that led to the eventual formulation of both his ultimate concern and pattern of ultimacy.

THEORETICAL WRITINGS (1914-1920)

Jung published two articles in 1914, both of which were further attempts to clarify his differences with Freud.[16] The first, "On Psychological Understanding," was a lecture delivered to the Psycho-Medical Society in London in which Jung distinguished between two approaches to understanding psychic contents: the analytical-reductive and the synthetic-constructive methods.[17] Jung identifies the former approach with Freud and the latter method with himself. Whereas Freud's method, according to Jung, is a retrospective approach that seeks the cause of neuroses in past events, the constructive method views psychic contents as having a teleological orientation, that is, as indicators of future psychic development. This does not mean, however, that the past should be ignored, but that both perspectives are needed to provide a unified understanding of the psyche. "The psyche is the point of intersection, hence it must be defined under two aspects. On the one hand it gives a picture of the remnants and traces of all that has been, and, on the other hand, . . . the outlines of what is to come."[18]

In particular, Jung argues that the teleological significance of psychic phenomena is especially evident in the fantasy systems of dementia patients. Jung sees in such fantasies the "desire to create a new world-system or what we call a *Weltanschauung*."[19] Peter Homans observes that this process is quite similar to the one Jung was experiencing during his crisis, in that he too was trying to find meaning in the fantasies he encountered in order to construct a new world view.[20]

This same theme is continued in the second article from 1914,"On the Importance of the Unconscious in Psychopathology."[21] After examining the role of unconscious material in cases of neuroses and psychoses, Jung concludes that delusions and hallucinations are found not only "in certain functional disturbances, . . . but also in normal people."[22] He explains that when the balance between consciousness and the unconscious is disturbed the unconscious contents break through into consciousness. Jung maintains, though, that the purpose of these fantasies is not to disturb consciousness but to compensate an imbalance in the conscious attitude. But not realizing the teleological nature of the fantasies, the individual fights against their intrusion into consciousness, which only increases the flow of unconscious material into consciousness and further disrupts conscious functioning. And when the compensating influence of the unconscious is completely ignored a neurosis or a psychosis develops. Given the previous discussion of Jung's encounter with his own unconscious, it is not surprising that he proposes an active engagement with the fantasy material as a solution to this problem. Jung would have more to say about this procedure in his 1916 article, "The Transcendent Function."[23]

In this article Jung focuses on the unitary nature of the psyche, or more precisely, on the "union of conscious and un-conscious contents."[24] It also should be noted that the term "transcendent" is not used in a strict metaphysical sense but simply denotes the "transition from one attitude to another."[25] Accordingly, the transcendent function can be thought of as an expanded attitude that includes both the conscious and the unconscious mind.

In Jung's view, the cultivation of an exclusively conscious attitude toward life, together with the suppression of the unconscious, results in the fragmentation of the psyche. Obviously, then, any rapprochement with consciousness necessitates a recognition of the unconscious and its contents, especially in the form of dreams and fantasy images; that is, it is only by actively engaging the material of the unconscious that one is able to redress the one-sided conscious standpoint. Following the method he outlined in his autobiography, Jung suggests taking a fantasy image and concentrating on it until the image is raised out of the unconscious to a position closer to con-sciousness. Once the content enters consciousness the next step is "to understand the meaning of the unconscious product."[26] Beyond that, the ego must then find a way to assimilate the unconscious content into consciousness, which is particularly difficult because the ego is the center of consciousness whereas the fantasy is a product of the unconscious, and there is a natural antagonism between the two realms.

For this procedure to succeed, then, it is essential that the two realms meet on equal footing, neither side dominating the other. Once this occurs, one can proceed with the process of interaction by initiating a dialogue between the ego and the fantasy image. In that dialogue, the two parties argue, discuss, and evaluate the viewpoint of the other, just "as if a dialogue were taking place between two human beings with equal rights."[27] This exchange between the ego and the fantasy image leads to a "third thing" that bridges the opposed positions and creates a new attitude consisting of consciousness and the unconscious. In Jung's view, when this process is successful a far reaching transformation of the personality occurs, affecting all aspects of life. "At all events the treatment of neurosis is not a kind of psychological water cure but a renewal of the personality, working in every direction and penetrating every sphere of life."[28] This is not, however, a one-time process, but an ongoing work having for its goal the continual increase of consciousness.

Jung's attempt to formulate a system uniquely his own took another major step forward in the 1916 publication "The Conception of the Unconscious."[29] Not only does this article build on the ideas found in "The Transcendent Function" but it also provides the basic structure for the individuation process; indeed, the term *individuation* appears for the first time in this article. The basis for understanding this preliminary formulation of the individuation process is Jung's distinction between the personal and collective unconscious. Here he describes the contents of the personal unconscious: "The materials contained in this layer are of a personal kind, inasmuch as on the one hand they may be characterised as acquisitions of the individual existence, and on the other as psychological factors which might just as well be conscious."[30]

Jung, of course, has Freud's theory in mind with this definition of the unconscious, which attributes the cause of various mental disturbances to repressed material from one's personal past. But in addition to this personally acquired layer of the psyche, Jung posits the existence of a deeper, collective layer, which is the "fundamental structure underlying every personality."[31] Sometimes, however, during the course of analysis this collective layer intrudes into consciousness, smothering the individual aspects of the personality. In response to this danger, the therapist must seek to foster the individual, rather than the collective qualities of the analysand, a process Jung calls "the way of individuation."

In another 1916 article, "Adaptation, Individuation, Collectivity," Jung again speaks of the concept of individuation.[32] He tells how individuation "cuts one off from personal conformity and hence from collectivity," and how a person must create an alternate, individually based value system in lieu of the values of the prevailing social order.[33] "He must offer a ransom in place of himself, that is, he must bring forth values which are an equivalent substitute for his absence in the collective sphere."[34] If replacement values are not formed, a tremendous sense of guilt arises from having renounced the values of the social order. In Jung's view the only means to expiate this guilt is by creating a new value system in place of the old one.

Clearly, then, the primary goal of individuation is the transformation of the psyche, not adaptation to outer, social reality. But this conflict between the individual and society results in intense isolation, suffering, and alienation in which one experiences the contempt of society.[35] "Thereby and at the same time he also separates himself from society. Outwardly he plunges into solitude, but inwardly into hell."[36] Paradoxically, though, this withdrawal from society is the basis for the creation of a new set of values possessing collective validity. "Every living creature that is able freely to develop itself individually . . . will through the perfecting of its individuality, soonest realize the ideal type of its species, . . . and will have collective validity."[37] So, rather than simply envisioning individuation as a narcissistic pursuit of "self," Jung understands it as the basis of social concern; that is, it is only by first developing oneself that a person can then expect to benefit society. "In this sense analysis is not a method that is a medical monopoly, but rather an art or technique or science of psychological life, which he who has been cured must continue to foster, for the sake of his own welfare and that of his environment."[38] As this quote clearly indicates, Jung attributes a heightened importance to the process of psychic development; instead of a process designed to remove temporary obstacles to adaptation, it is presented here as an ongoing way of life.

In the 1917 essay "The Psychology of the Unconscious Processes," Jung continued mapping out the contours of his newly emerging system.[39] By this time he had weathered the worst part of his crisis and he was now beginning to formulate a coherent theoretical structure to explain his experiences. He begins the essay with a statement that reveals a major change in his attitude toward the study of the psyche.

> Hence it comes about that the inquirer after the secrets of the human soul, learns rather less than nothing from experimental

psychology. He would be better advised to abandon exact science, take off his scholar's gown, say farewell to his study, and then . . . , set out to wander through the world.[40]

Although Jung had began his career as an experimental psychologist, he is here strongly criticizing this method as a viable way to study the psyche. This refutation sets the agenda for the remainder of the essay, containing as it does the outlines of Jung's new approach to the psyche.

In this essay, Jung divides his work of the past years into five stages. The first stage consists of his analysis of the theories of Freud and Adler, both of which he views as reductionistic: Freud reducing psychic existence to sexuality, and Adler reducing it to the "will to power." As for Freud's theory, Jung claims that despite its "one-sidedness", it is "right up to a certain point."[41] Likewise he gives Adler's theory partial credit, particularly his teleological view of neuroses. Jung's central concern, however, is to evaluate the truth claims of these two theories, which leads him to the second stage of his work.

In an attempt to account for the differences between Freud and Adler's positions, Jung equates each of these theories with "two opposite psychological types."[42] "The first we called the extraverted type, because in the main he goes outside himself to the object, the latter is called the introverted type, because in a major degree he turns away from the object, withdrawing into himself and thinking about it."[43] Jung classifies Freud's theory as extraverted and Adler's theory as introverted. Depending on the nature of any given case, either the Freudian or the Adlerian position may be applicable; but, according to Jung, in no circumstance is either theory applicable in all cases.

Hence the third stage in the evolution of Jung's thought consists in the formulation of an alternate theory in place of those provided by Freud and Adler. By contrast to Freud's view of sexual conflict and Adler's theory of inferiority, Jung proposes a "typological" theory centering on the conflict between the adapted function and the undifferentiated co-function.[44] Specifically, in the case of the introvert the conflict is between thinking and unconscious feeling, whereas the reverse is true for the extravert. A conflict between functions is most noticeable and serious when a person confronts a situation requiring use of the undeveloped function. At such times the required use of the inferior function, owing to its undeveloped nature, may result in an inability to perform or to judge a given situation properly. More will be said about Jung's theory of types when we discuss his 1921 work devoted to this subject.[45] At this time, the theory is still in an early stage of development.

The fourth component in the formation of Jung's thought concerns the relationship between the unconscious and the phenomenon of the transference. In simplest terms transference refers to the "projection of unconscious contents onto the analyst."[46] The first stage of this phenomenon, which results in the projection of personal contents onto the analyst so that he appears, for example, as a father-figure or lover, is a matter of common occurrence in both Freudian and Jungian analysis, and is typically resolved by analyzing the underlying infantile causes of the projections. However, in Jungian analysis, other fantasies appear having nothing to do with personal reminiscences; no longer viewed as father or lover, "the physician now appears to be endowed with uncanny qualities; he may be either a wizard or a demoniacal criminal, or his counterpart of virtue, a saviour. Later on he appears as an incomprehensible mixture of both sides."[47] These figures are projections from the impersonal (collective) unconscious rather than the personal unconscious, and ordinarily appear after the resolution of the personal projections.

Jung explains that after dissolving the personal projections, the libido previously invested in them sinks into the depths of the unconscious, where it revives the impersonal contents.[48] When these powerful unconscious images are activated, they are either projected onto the analyst or introjected and attributed to oneself. So, in order to avoid either extreme, Jung encourages the analysand to "separate himself from the unconscious—not by repressing it, for then it seizes him from behind—but by presenting it visibly to himself as something that is totally different from him."[49] This means that the ego must be separated from what Jung calls the "non-ego" so that the projected unconscious material can be reclaimed as part of a larger psychic totality. Jung warns, however, that for this endeavor to succeed one needs a well-developed ego in order to withstand the incursion of the unconscious material; otherwise there is the danger that this material may completely overwhelm the conscious standpoint and cause a psychosis.

The transcendent function or fifth component of Jung's new system, as previously noted, is the name given to the "function" that bridges the unconscious and conscious mind.[50] In the analytical setting, the transcendent function is most relevant when the analysand is confronting images from the collective unconscious, since the goal at that time is to raise the images of the collective unconscious to consciousness so that a working relationship can be established with them. Jung describes what is gained from this process: "An enrichment of the individual is attained by this compensatory process, giving him greater decision and the possibility of a harmony that is complete in itself."[51] Thus, the transcendent function has a transforming effect on the psyche, significantly widening the domain of consciousness and providing an increased degree of psychic wholeness.

PSYCHOLOGICAL TYPES

Jung's next major work during this period was the 1921 publication of *Psychological Types*.[52] This work is an important link in the formulation of the individuation process, as is evidenced by the book's original subtitle, *The Psychology of Individuation*. But the majority of Jung's discussion is devoted to a historical survey of previous typological theories. For the most part, though, that need not concern us here since our interest is with the formulation of Jung's ultimate concern. In this work, Jung puts forth—albeit in a rather unsystematic way— the unification of the psyche as his ultimate concern. Although existing in a preliminary and, at times, vague form, we can nonetheless discern the emerging outlines of his religious goal. Still, it would be another seven years before Jung fully and clearly articulated the seminal thoughts found in this work.

Previously, Jung had differentiated between introverted and extroverted types, proposing that the libido of the extravert is directed outward towards objects, while the interest of the introvert is directed inward toward the subject.[53] Based on that distinction, Jung now expands his type theory to include four psychological functions: thinking, feeling, sensation, and intuition. Although each function can be either introverted or extraverted, usually one function and one type, such as thinking/ introvert or feeling/extravert, predominates one's personality, while the opposite or inferior function, because of disuse, sinks into the unconscious where it causes a variety of psychological disturbances.[54] At the same time, though, this function, because of its proximity to the unconscious, serves as a link between consciousness and the unconscious.

To set the stage for his discussion of psychic unity, Jung first addresses the issue of psychic fragmentation. In terms of the type theory, Jung claims that life becomes one-dimensional (and hence fragmented) when the dominant function rules the psyche to the exclusion of the other functions. In particular, he believes that since the "thinking" function dominates modern culture, the inferior function (in this case feeling) becomes "an ever-bleeding wound in the psyche of modern man."[55] Hence over-identification with the dominant function results in a loss of selfhood, in that a person is reduced to one aspect of a larger psychic totality. And since the social order encourages this over-identification by its extreme emphasis on rationality, the other functions are repressed in response to this collective mandate. Unfortunately, though, the values of the collective are only penultimate in comparison to the "higher" individual values which lie hidden below the inferior function.

> It may well be that beneath the neglected function there lie hidden far higher individual values which, though of small importance for collective life, are of the greatest value for individual life, and are therefore vital values that can endow the life of the individual with an intensity and beauty he will vainly seek in his collective function.[56]

In other words, individual values take precedence over collective ones. Thus, by siding with the individual rather than the collective, Jung ends up locating the higher individual values within the unconscious; that is, in the final analysis "it is the contents of the unconscious that have the supreme power," not the values of the social order.[57]

Since the inferior function provides access to the unconscious, it is necessary to develop this function in order to reach these higher values.

> In psychological terms, the functions that have lain fallow and unfertile, and were unused, repressed, undervalued, despised, etc., suddenly burst forth and begin to live. It is precisely the least valued function that enables life, which was threatened with extinction by the differentiated function, to continue.[58]

Until the inferior function is reclaimed, the individual leads a fractured existence, cut off from a deeper source of psychic unity and meaning. But as soon as one comes to terms with the inferior function, "a symbol . . . arise[s] which . . . express[es] his accomplished destiny, i. e., his individual way on which the Yea and Nay are united."[59] Here, for the first time, Jung explicitly connects the fulfillment of the individual's destiny with the reconciliation of psychic opposites. Psychologically, this symbol "embraces both conscious and unconscious," thereby unifying the fragmented psyche into a larger totality. Expressed in terms of the type theory, Jung was seeking a principle capable of forming a psychic totality among the diverse psychic "functions." For the sake of clarity, I will quote Jung in length.

> We are therefore compelled to acknowledge that the universality of our ideal is a limitation, and to look round for a *spiritus rector* which, bearing in mind the claims of a fuller life, can offer us a greater guarantee of psychological universality than the intellect alone can encompass. When Faust exclaims "feeling is all," he is expressing merely the antithesis of the intellect, and so only goes to the other extreme; he does not achieve that totality of life and of his own psyche in which feeling and thinking are united in a third and higher principle.[60]

The inner psychic unity to which Jung refers results from an intense introversion of libido which activates the unconscious contents. Jung compares this condition to the practice of *yoga*, where attention is systematically withdrawn from the outer to the inner world, and to the unity of opposites found in various Indian and Chinese concepts, such as the *tat tvam asi* (that art thou) of the Upanishads and the *Tao* of the *Tao-Te-Ching*.[61]

For Jung these concepts function as metaphors for a "middle way" unifying the psychic opposites. He is thus using these terms divested of their traditional metaphysical connotations; instead he is using them to describe a psychological condition of unity and those "laws" governing the inner world of the psyche.

> The natural flow of libido, this same middle path, means complete obedience to the fundamental laws of human nature, and there can be no higher moral principle than harmony with natural laws that guide the libido in the direction of life's optimum. . . . The optimum can be reached only through obedience to the tidal laws of the libido . . . laws which . . . set us those individual life tasks without whose accomplishment the vital optimum can never be attained.[62]

Because this "inner Tao" directs life and the flow of psychic energy to its completest fulfillment, it is imperative to follow this inner principle if one hopes to live a harmonious and unified existence. The basis for this harmonious existence is the unification of the psyche. "The saving factor is the symbol, which embraces both conscious and unconscious and unites them. . . . At all events the appearance of the redeeming symbol is closely connected with destruction and devastation. If the old were not ripe for death, nothing new would appear."[63] Although Jung does not tell us specifically what this unifying symbol is, he does mention that it is located in the unconscious, and that it signals the beginning of a new way of life.

Despite taking a substantial step forward in the formulation of his ultimate concern, a certain vagueness still exists. For instance, Jung has not yet settled on a definite formulation for this "third thing," other than calling it an "individual nucleus."[64] This "third thing," which unites the opposites and provides access to the "higher" individual values, is also synonymous with a person's individuality. In addition, Jung equates this "third thing" with the "highest value, the highest ideal."[65] In still yet another passage, Jung calls this reconcilor of opposites the self, and differentiates it from ego-consciousness by locating it in the depths of the unconscious. "For this we must go deeper; we must descend into the foundations of consciousness which have still preserved their primordial instinctivity—that is, into the unconscious, . . . "[66]

Furthermore, Jung calls this nucleus an "authority we have to appeal to, since it is a neutral region of the psyche where everything that is divided and antagonistic in consciousness flows together into groupings and configurations."[67] These configurations occupy an "independent middle position" between consciousness and the unconscious, allowing for a unification of the two standpoints. But more importantly, Jung bestows upon the unconscious and its contents a supreme worth. Unfortunately, though, due to its seemingly irrational nature, this important sphere of life has been repressed; now, however, with the lifting of this repression through analysis, "what was once despised becomes the supreme principle, and what was once truth now becomes error. This reversal of values is similar to the devastation of a country by floods."[68]

Jung speaks of the birth of this new source of value and meaning in terms of the "god image," which he defines as the "collective expression of the most overwhelmingly powerful influence exerted on the conscious mind by unconscious concentrations of libido."[69] He cautions, though, that this image is simply one of many images found in the unconscious and should not be confused with any metaphysical or theological conception of God. Most people, however, wrongly project this energy outward upon objects, conferring an unwarranted power upon them.

> Psychologically, this means that when the libido invested in God, i.e., the surplus value that has been projected, is recognized as a projection, the object loses its overpowering significance, and the surplus value consequently accrues to the individual, giving rise to a feeling of intense vitality, or new potential. . . . It is as though the supreme value were shifted elsewhere so that it is now found inside and not outside.[70]

But, as Jung indicates, when these projections are withdrawn, the energy formerly invested in them returns to the psyche, and instills it with the "highest value."

This shift of value has a transforming effect on life, infusing it with new-found meaning and significance. No longer is ultimate meaning found in either the gods or society; it is found in the individual psyche. The "supreme," the "ultimate," that which unifies the psyche, all these are found within the depths of the unconscious. The unconscious is the locus of ultimate meaning, containing as it does a wealth of potential that up to now has laid dormant.

> A new and powerful life springs up just where there had seemed to be no life and no power and no possibility of further development. It comes streaming out of the unconscious, from that unknown part of the psyche which is treated as nothing by all rationalists. From this discredited and rejected region comes the new afflux of energy, the renewal of life.[71]

The process leading to the cultivation of this dormant potential, as well as the unification of the psyche, is known as the way of individuation. We now turn to an examination of this process.

Chapter Five

Individuation of the Self
as Ultimate Concern

A ll the existing evidence indicates that by 1919 the intensity of Jung's crisis experience was over. Through his work with his fantasies he had begun the process of formulating the pattern of his new ultimate concern. In the conclusion of "The Psychology of the Unconscious Processes" Jung describes the outcome of his confrontation with the unconscious:

> I lay myself open to adverse criticism, because I conceive it to be the duty of every one who isolates himself by taking his own path, to tell others what he has found or discovered, whether it be a refreshing spring for the thirsty, or a sandy desert of sterile error. . . . Our age is seeking a new spring of life. I found one and drank of it and the water tasted good. That is all I can or want to say.[1]

But Jung would in fact have much more to say in the years ahead, for this statement signifies a major turning point in his life. After all the years of struggle and conflict, Jung finally found a new source of ultimacy; no longer able to rely on organized belief systems, or Freudian analysis, Jung's religious goal was grounded in the direct experience of his own psyche. As we will see, it was the self and its realization that finally provided "the spring of life" he was seeking. The theoretical formulation of his discovery became his chief task between the years 1922 and 1928.

During the following years Jung's work moved in two directions: on the one hand, he addressed himself to various cultural and psychological issues such as marriage, education, psychotherapy, and child development, while on the other hand, he continued his formulation of the individuation process. The clearest and fullest expression of the individuation process during this period is found in the *Two Essays on Analytical Psychology*.[2] The first essay, initially published in 1912 as "New Paths in Psychology," was revised and expanded for its 1917 publication as "The Psychology of the Unconscious Processes."[3] It then appeared in 1928 with further revisions to form the first part of the *Two Essays on Analytical Psychology* under the new title, "On the Psychology of the Unconscious."[4]

Similarly, the second essay underwent a number of major revisions. Initially appearing in 1916 as "The Structure of the Unconscious," it was later expanded to its 1928 form entitled "The Relations Between the Ego and the Unconscious."[5] This latter essay forms the basis for the better part of the following discussion. I will, however, supplement this work by use of other relevant contemporaneous documentation.

THE PSYCHIC STRUCTURE

Since individuation involves a fundamental restructuring of the human mind, it is necessary to begin our investigation by first clarifying Jung's understanding of the psyche. This will allow us to understand why he felt that this process was such a "vital necessity and an unavoidable task in the education of the human race."[6] As previously mentioned, Jung divided the mind into a conscious and unconscious sphere, with the unconscious further divided into a personal and collective layer. The personal unconscious includes material acquired during this lifetime such as forgotten or repressed material as well as material too weak to enter directly into consciousness. In addition to these personal acquisitions, there exist contents that are universal and timeless, the mythological images of the collective unconscious. Their source is the "inherited brain-structure itself," which shapes these images according to certain archetypal patterns.[7]

The relationship between consciousness and the unconscious is compensatory, in that any one-sidedness in consciousness is balanced by an opposite reaction in the unconscious.[8] The unconscious accomplishes its work by the production of fantasies and dream images, which not only balance consciousness but also serve as the basis for our conscious experience of reality. "What indeed is reality if it is not a reality in ourselves, an *esse in anima*. . . . The psyche creates reality every day. The only expression I can use for this activity is fantasy."[9] The center of consciousness which experiences the contents of the unconscious is known as the ego.

In the early years of life, consciousness is still not fully developed, nor is there an ego to provide continuity to awareness. But gradually, as ego-consciousness evolves out of the unconscious, the child begins to speak in terms of "I." As development continues, the ego begins to differentiate itself from the unconscious, until ego-consciousness is firmly established. The first stage of this process consists of the ability to make "mere connections between two or more psychic contents," although memory of these connections is not yet established.[10] Additional development results in awareness of subjective elements and a recognition that these subjective contents belong to oneself. And finally, when the ego becomes fully separated from its state of primordial unity with the unconscious, an experience of "I-ness" or ego-consciousness arises.[11]

The birth of ego-consciousness results in a bifurcation of the psyche so that the world is experienced as distinct from oneself. Jung designates this distinct sense of "I-ness" as the ego: "By ego I understand a complex of ideas which constitutes the centre of my field of consciousness and appears to possess a high degree of continuity and identity."[12] Whereas consciousness is composed of feelings, thoughts, fantasies, and perceptions, the ego is what allows awareness of these contents to take place. In other words, the ego is both the "organ of awareness" of the contents of consciousness and the process by which consciousness is organized. In and of itself the ego serves a positive function in the psyche: it provides a sense of continuity to one's experience; allows for an awareness of the contents of consciousness; and organizes consciousness into a coherent structure.

Whereas the ego is the center of consciousness, the self is the center of the psyche in its totality and the basis of identity. Accordingly, the ego is subordinate to the self in the larger framework of the total personality structure. The self, however, is not an identity that one creates; rather, the self is inherent—albeit in a latent form—within one's psychic makeup. "Individuation, therefore, can only mean a process of psychological development that fulfills the individual qualities given; in other words, it is a process by which a man becomes the definite, unique being he in fact is."[13]

The point is that the self is not fabricated or constructed but is discovered or realized in the course of the analytical process. Jung goes on to caution, though, that the self, because it is an archetype, is not known directly. According to Jung, an archetype is a model which gives rise to certain psychic images or symbols; although the archetypes are not perceived directly, their symbolic manifestations are. More exactly, then, the self is the archetype of unity and wholeness of the entire psychic system, and, as such, is the expression of one's uniqueness and individuality. The self in this capacity serves to unify the entire personality—both consciousness and the unconscious—into a coherent whole.[14] In addition, the self plays a compensatory role in the psyche, so that whenever an imbalance occurs in one's conscious orientation, the self will take steps (dreams, fantasies, conflicts) to redress the imbalance and reestablish psychic equilibrium. It does this by producing symbols and images, which evoke strong emotionally toned experiences capable of transforming the overall personality structure.

Closely related to the ego is the persona which Jung defined as "a functional complex that comes into existence for reasons of adaptation" [to the external world].[15] As the word indicates, the persona refers to a "mask" which one adopts in response to the performance of social duties and roles; it is, accordingly, a collective identity founded on cultural values and standards.[16] The construction of a workable persona is, of course, a necessary part of human development, since a person must "internalize the collective ideals or collective consciousness of the community" in order to function within society.[17] But because the persona is a socially fabricated form of identity, it is void of any basis other than social and cultural convention.[18]

> Fundamentally the persona is nothing real: it is a compromise
> between individual and society as to what a man should appear
> to be. He takes a name, earns a title, exercises a function, he is
> this or that. In a certain sense all this is real, yet in relation to
> the essential individuality of the person concerned it is only a
> secondary reality. . . . [19]

As a social tool the persona is useful, but, in Jung's view, it
is insufficient as the basis for an authentic form of selfhood.[20]

Thus when a person's identity is established by recourse to
such criteria as social status, wealth, occupation, title, and rep-
utation, a "feigned" individuality develops.

> Identification with one's office or one's title is very attractive
> indeed, which is precisely why so many men are nothing more
> than the decorum accorded to them by society. In vain would
> one look for a personality behind the husk.'. . . That is why
> the office—or whatever this outer husk may be—is so attrac-
> tive: it offers easy compensation for personal deficiencies.[21]

In Jung's view, the problem can be conceived as a case of mistaken identity caused by the ego's identification with the persona. The inflated ego is thereby elevated to the center of one's
psychic life where it functions as the basis for identity; but as
mentioned, the persona is a social fabrication, and lacks the
necessary substance on which to build a meaningful and lasting
sense of selfhood.[22]

Jung argues that a number of psychological repercussions
result from the ego's mistaken identification with the persona.
First, since the collective nature of the persona is antithetical to
one's own unique form of individuality, this discrepancy may
cause a variety of problems.[23] The main problem, however,
with the ego's identification with the persona is that a considerable amount of psychic energy is required to maintain this
identity structure. Because of this, there is a need to be constantly
"on guard" so that nothing can get through to call the existence
of the persona into question. In Jung's words, "these purely
'personal' people are always very sensitive, for something may

easily happen that will bring into consciousness an unwelcome portion of their real ('individual') character."[24] Consequently, there is a tendency to become rigid, and in many cases, there is an inability to experience life fully and directly. The mainte- nance of the persona, moreover, requires the censoring of life in accordance with the contour of one's self-created image; certain aspects of external reality as well as a whole range of internal contents must be ignored. But by far the greatest travesty is the suppression of one's unique form of individuality in deference to the collective ideals of the persona. In Jung's view "far too much of our common humanity has to be sacrificed in the interests of an ideal image into which one tries to mould oneself."[25] In short, then, although the persona provides a cer- tain understanding of one's role in life, a high price is exacted for this gain.

The problem, psychologically viewed, is that when the ego assumes itself to be the center of the psyche, the self begins to react to its own repressed condition.

> Despite the exclusive identity of the ego-consciousness with the persona the unconscious self, one's real individuality, is always present and makes itself felt indirectly if not directly. Although the ego-consciousness is at first identical with the persona—that compromise role in which we parade before the community—yet the unconscious self can never be re- pressed to the point of extinction.[26]

But despite the disturbing effect of the unconscious contents on consciousness, the ego generally ignores these warnings, until the tension between consciousness and the unconscious can no longer be tolerated. At that point, depending on the strength and severity of the unconscious reaction, a neurosis or psycho- sis may occur.

PATTERN OF ULTIMACY

One of the goals of individuation, therefore, is to reestab- lish the severed link between the ego and self; as long as the two are unrelated there cannot be any psychic wholeness or harmony. But in order to establish a relationship between the ego and self, the ego must first be separated from its identification with the persona. Individuation thus begins with a critical evaluation of the persona in an attempt to free the ego from identification with collective values, the net effect of which is a dislodging of the ego as the basis of identity, and the implementation of the self to its rightful place as the center of the psyche.

The first step in the individuation process is to analyze the persona in order to free the ego from its identification with the collectivity. "When we analyse the persona we strip off the mask, and discover that what seemed to be individual is at bottom collective; in other words, that the persona was only a mask of the collective psyche."[27] Briefly stated, the analytical process consists of a variety of methods used to establish contact with the unconscious, including dream analysis, active imagination, analysis of the transference, and various artistic expressions.[28] Since the unconscious has a compensatory relationship to consciousness, and since conscious over-identification with the persona represents a psychic imbalance, the analyst assumes that dreams and other unconscious material will indicate this one-sidedness.

Through analysis, the analysand gains insight into the persona, whereby its absolute existence is called into question; that is, once it has been scrupulously analyzed, the persona eventually begins to collapse. Consequently, the psychic energy previously used to maintain it is released into the unconscious where it further activates the contents therein.[29] This new unconscious material confronts consciousness, further calling into question the seemingly absolute nature of the persona until it is finally seen for what it is—namely, a role masking one's true self.

With the pending breakdown of the persona one is thrown into the midst of an interior crisis marked by confusion and disorientation. As Jung states: "The forces that burst out of the collective psyche have a confusing and blinding effect."[30] Mental contents whose existence one had never before suspected now confront the ego, shaking the very foundation of its persona-based world view; no longer is the ego in control, since the unconscious now dominates it—admittedly in an uncontrolled and possibly dangerous way.[31] The ego, sensing the impending threat to the dissolution of the persona, tries to shore up the persona, but to no avail. And finally, when the tension and struggle can no longer be maintained, the persona succumbs to the pressure of the unconscious and collapses completely. Jung describes this state of affairs as "a condition of panic, a letting go in the face of apparently hopeless complications."[32] Peter Homans has also acknowledged the importance of the breakdown of the persona, describing it as the "typically Jungian moment in analysis."[33]

More exactly, not only does the breakdown of the persona represent an intense crisis experience in which one's entire world view has collapsed, but the supposed center of the psyche (the ego) has been displaced from its position of power. In the following quote Jung describes this psychic condition and the feelings it evokes.

> A collapse of the conscious attitude is no small matter. It always feels like the end of the world, as though everything had tumbled back into original chaos. One feels delivered up, disoriented, like a rudderless ship that is abandoned to the moods of the elements.[34]

That a person should undergo a crisis upon the breakdown of the persona is not surprising, since the persona had served as the basis of meaning and identity, both of which have now been undermined. There is, moreover, no longer a functioning psychic center to assume control of the psyche. Although the ego has been displaced by a power beyond its control (the unconscious), a new center (the self) has not yet been established.

From the standpoint of the ego, this entire experience is one of intense alienation and suffering. The old, familiar, dependable patterns of relating to the world are no longer functional. Whereas the previous ego-structure made for a secure and seemingly permanent sense of selfhood, here the exact opposite is true.[35]

> The predominance of unconscious influences, together with the associated disintegration of the persona and the deposition of the conscious mind from power, constitute a state of

> psychic disequilibrium which, in analytical treatment, is arti-
> ficially induced for the therapeutic purpose of resolving a
> difficulty that might block further development. . . . It often
> seems as though these patients had only been waiting to find a
> trustworthy person in order to give up and collapse.[36]

But despite the disorientation, ambiguity, and confusion, these experiences are a necessary part of the process of re-aligning the psychic structure. In other words, prior to recon-structing the psyche, a breakdown of the old structure must first occur. Jung mentions three possible alternatives for dealing with this breakdown: a regressive restoration of the persona to its pre-crisis state; an identification with the unconscious con-tents; or a confronting of the unconscious contents.[37] Jung advocates the last option which requires an acceptance of the meaning and identity void one is in. It is a void in the sense that the ego no longer has any point of reference in the overall psychic structure. On the one hand, it is buffeted about by seemingly strange and unknown contents stemming from the unconscious, while on the other hand, it is no longer able to identify with the collective ideals of the persona. All sense of place, purpose, meaning, and identity are suspended, leaving one in a state of total psychic chaos.

As confusing as this stage of the individuation process may be, still Jung believed that the situation was not totally hopeless.

> There is a destination, a possible goal, beyond the alternative
> stages [mentioned above]. That is the way of individuation.
> Individuation means becoming an "in-dividual," and, in so far
> as "individuality" embraces our innermost, last, and incom-
> parable uniqueness, it also implies becoming one's own self. We
> could therefore translate individuation as "coming to selfhood"
> [*Verselbstung*] or "self-realization" [*Selbstverwirklichung*].[38]

An additional prerequisite, however, for self-realization is that the ego (although now free from the persona) must still be freed from its association with the unconscious material, or in Jung's terms, the power of the unconscious—as it appears in its symbolic, archetypal form of the anima—must be assimilated. This marks the beginning of the reconstruction of the shattered psyche.

The anima, as Jung defines it, is the symbolic embodiment of all that is lacking in a man's conscious orientation toward life, and, as such, it can be thought of as the "inner personality" of the unconscious, containing "all those common human qualities" not found in consciousness.[39] Similarly, Jung used the term animus to symbolize the inner qualities of a woman's unconscious.[40] Whereas the anima symbolizes the feminine qualities of a man's unconscious, the animus symbolizes the masculine qualities of a woman's. The image of the anima is archetypal, in that it is a composite "of all the ancestral experiences of the female," or in the case of the animus, it is a composite of all ancestral experiences of the masculine.[41] In dreams the anima appears as a female figure while the animus takes the form of various masculine figures. In human relationships, these figures are usually projected onto the contrasexual partner, so that the woman becomes the bearer of a man's unconscious and the man the carrier of a woman's. These projections cause "an absolute affective tie" to the other person, as well as a variety of psychological and relationship problems.[42]

One establishes a relationship with the anima or animus by a two-part movement: a direct experiencing of the unconscious contents, and an active interpretation of them. "It is a question of releasing unconscious processes and letting them come into the conscious mind in the form of fantasies. We can try our hand at interpreting these fantasies if we like. . . . But it is of vital importance that he should experience them to the full. . . ."[43] Direct experience is of primary importance at this juncture, since any understanding of the unconscious presupposes a relationship with its contents. This is accomplished by allowing the fantasies of the unconscious to enter consciousness so that an ongoing dialogue can be established with them. This assumes, of course, that the ego has sufficient strength to engage in such an undertaking; otherwise the unconscious contents may completely overwhelm consciousness.

Specifically (in the anima's case), the goal of this dialectical process is to free the ego from the power of the anima and to establish a working relationship with the unconscious. The first step consists of objectifying the anima by actively engaging in a dialogue with her. For example, after asking a question of the anima, one then allows an answer to arise from the unconscious. As Jung explains: "The art of it consists only in allowing our invisible partner to make herself heard, in putting the mechanism of expression momentarily at her disposal. . . . "[44] Whereas all criticism is withheld while the anima is speaking, once she is through, then the process of interpretation and judgement can begin.[45] The objectification of the unconscious content has a depotentiating effect on the anima; instead of the mood or image unconsciously disrupting consciousness, it ceases to do so when it is made the object of one's attention. For this to work, however, one must take the fantasy seriously, assigning to the unconscious an "absolute reality."[46] According to Jung, the fantasy "is an expression, an appearance standing for something unknown but real."[47] Although initially this means that the fantasy should be' taken literally, after experiencing the image it should once again be viewed as a symbol of a psychic nature.

The immediate outcome of interacting with the anima is the transformation of this image from an antagonistic figure into a "function of relationship between consciousness and the unconscious."[48] Rather than disrupting consciousness with moods and fantasies, the anima now facilitates the process of conscious/unconscious interaction, thus decreasing, or at least regulating, the flow of disruptive elements into consciousness. Accordingly, the conscious domain is progressively enlarged by the addition of new unconscious material, until finally a radical transformation of the overall personality structure occurs, and a new relationship with the unconscious is established.[49]

Subsequent to coming to terms with the anima, the ego experiences a new sense of strength, which gives rise to still yet another archetypal image—namely, the "mana-personality."[50] The mana-personality is an image of the "mighty man in the form of hero, chief, magician, medicine-man, saint, the ruler of men and spirits."[51] For a woman, the mana-personality is symbolized by the "Great Mother, the All-Merciful, who understands everything, forgives everything, who always acts for the best, living only for others."[52] Psychologically speaking, these figures possess the power (mana) previously attributed to the unconscious (anima). In and of itself the mana-personality does not present a problem. But if the ego should identify with it—as it inevitably does—then the ego becomes inflated. Conversely, if one concretizes the mana-personality as an "extramundane 'Father in Heaven'," then the ego is undervalued.[53] In both cases a problem arises because of the ego's mistaken belief that it has conquered the unconscious. "The ego has appropriated something that does not belong to it. ... Hence we must conclude that the ego never conquered the anima at all and therefore has not acquired the mana."[54] Instead of conquering the anima, the ego has simply become adulterated by the power of the mana-personality; as long as the ego remains in this deluded state of association with the mana-personality, the unconscious will continue to inflate the ego.

For Jung, the solution to this problem is for the ego to "drop its claim to victory" over the anima by realizing that it cannot dominate the unconscious.[55] In response, the mana-personality will release the ego from its grip. Here again it is necessary to experience this image and to take a discriminating attitude toward it; by so doing, the ego is able to disentangle itself from the mana-personality just as it did with the anima. "In differentiating the ego from the archetype of the mana-personality one is now forced, exactly as in the case of the anima, to make conscious those contents which are specific of the mana-personality."[56] Characteristic of the mana-personality is its seemingly "superior wisdom" and "will to power," qualities which are responsible for the ego's inflated condition. But once these qualities are experienced and understood as not belonging to the ego, the mana-personality relinquishes its hold. The ego, now freed from the influence of this figure, is ready for its confrontation with the self.

With the demise of the mana-personality, neither the ego nor the unconscious has ultimate power over the other. Rather, the mana's power has fallen to a psychic point located midway between conscious and the unconscious. "This something is the desired 'mid-point' of the personality, that ineffable something betwixt the opposites, or else that which unites them, or the result of conflict, or the product of energetic tension: the coming to birth of personality, a profoundly individual step forward. ... "[57] Since the ego is now free from the influence of both the persona and the unconscious, it is able to confront the unconscious on equal footing, which in turn establishes a new psychic equilibrium consisting of both a conscious and unconscious component. This new psychic center is the self.[58]

Psychologically, the confrontation of the ego with the self is experienced as a power or force beyond the control of the conscious mind. In Jung's view, this confrontation with the unknown and indefinable self has a transforming effect on the psyche. Jung goes on to describe the self as the "God within us," by which he does not mean a "deification of man or a dethronement of God."[59] Such responses typify the ego in the previous mana stage of development; rather Jung uses the term "God" as a means to describe the ego's experience of the self.

> If we leave the idea of "divinity" out of account and speak only of "autonomous contents," we maintain a position that is intellectually and empirically correct. . . . By using the concept of a divine being we give apt expression to the peculiar way in which we experience the workings of the autonomous contents. . . . Therefore, by affixing the attribute "divine" to the workings of autonomous contents, we are admitting their relatively superior force.[60]

Whereas the ego in its pre-individuated state experienced itself as the subjective center of the psyche, the ego is now experienced as an object by the self, the new center of the psyche. That is to say, from the vantage point of the ego's subordinate position in the psyche, it is now accessible, as it were, to the influence of the self, which the ego experiences as a mysterious and powerful "other."

In addition, Jung understands the self as the focal point and goal of personality development.[61] As previously mentioned, to become an individual means, among other things, to differentiate oneself from collective norms and to become a unique human being. In Jung's words, then, "individuation . . . is a process of differentiation, having for its goal the development of the individual personality."[62] This development is not simply a penultimate therapeutic concern, but a "prime necessity" and an "indispensable requirement."[63] Jung emphasizes the crucial importance of individuation when he writes: "Individuation is indispensable for certain people, not only as a therapeutic necessity, but as a high ideal, an idea of the best we can do."[64] This goal, in the form of the self-realization process, functions as Jung's ultimate concern as well as his ideal image of what it means to be a full human being; that is, once the self is realized, the ultimate aim and purpose of life is fulfilled. As Jung puts it: "So too the self is our life's goal, for it is the completest expression of that fateful combination we call individuality."[65]

SUMMARY

Thus, we can make the following observation about Jung's religious goal: Jung's avoidance of externalizing the psychological experience of the self allows us to classify his ultimate concern as nontranscendent. In other words, Jung does not objectify the self by giving it an ontological status as a deity existing "out there." Instead, he limits his claims to the realm of the psyche; individuation of the self is the goal of human life, and the source of ultimate meaning. "One could not go beyond the center. The center is the goal, and everything is directed toward that center. . . . The self is the principle and archetype of orientation and meaning."[66]

With the "realization of the self" we reach the end of the individuation process; the consolidation of Jung's ultimate concern is now complete. Describing the importance of the self, Jung wrote: "I knew that in finding the mandala as an expression of the self I had attained what was for me the ultimate. Perhaps someone else knows more, but not I."[67] He has, moreover, clearly articulated his pattern of ultimacy in the form of the individuation process. Beginning with the breakdown of the persona, the involvement with the anima/animus, the demise of the mana figure, and finally the confrontation with the self, Jung formulated the stages leading to psychic wholeness. But despite the self's power to unify the psyche and endow life with meaning, Jung still viewed the individual as separate from the world at large. We now turn to an examination of the elaboration of both his ultimate concern and pattern of ultimacy.

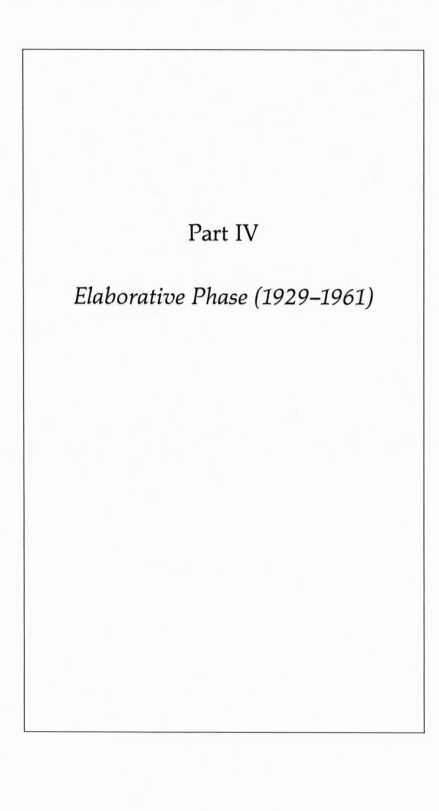

Part IV

Elaborative Phase (1929–1961)

Chapter Six

Symbols of Ultimacy

By 1928 Jung had formulated his ultimate concern as well as his pattern of ultimacy, and he would now spend the remainder of his life elaborating these initial formulations. Although his ultimate concern (the quest for wholeness) remained intact, he did expand his understanding of wholeness to include the unity of the human psyche with the universe at large; but rather than a radical change in ultimacy, this modification represents an expansion of his ultimate concern to cosmic proportions. The self, rather than simply the unifier of the psyche, is capable of reconciling all opposites, including mind and matter into a larger totality. Likewise Jung modified his pattern of ultimacy, adding some new elements and downplaying previous components. Most notably, the notion of the persona ceased to play a central role in the individuation process, while the archetype of the shadow gained in prominence.

As a means to elaborate his religious goal, Jung broadened his researches into a variety of cultural domains. It was during this period that Jung's major works on culture, religion, therapy, alchemy, mythology, and personality development were written. Since it is obviously beyond the scope of this study to treat Jung's thoughts on these subjects in full, I will broach these topics to the extent that they shed light on the elaboration of his ultimate concern.

I have divided the elaborative phase of Jung's life into two sections. The chapter entitled "Symbols of Ultimacy" extends from 1929 to 1943 and consists of a period of increased public visibility and notoriety. The chapter on "Alchemy and Whole-ness" runs from 1944 to 1961 and is dominated by the publica-tion of Jung's alchemical works. Through an examination of each of these two periods, my aim is to show how Jung ampli-fied, and in some cases modified, his ultimate concern and pat-tern of ultimacy.

By contrast to the relatively solitary and turbulent nature of the preceding years, Jung entered into a period of increased public involvement. He began his reentry into society by con-vening his English seminars in Zurich, something he had not done since 1925.[1] These seminars, which began in 1928 and continued until 1939, served as a forum for Jung's new ideas. In addition to consolidating a small but committed group of fol-lowers in Zurich, Jung's work was beginning to receive world-wide recognition. In 1933 he became president of the Interna-tional General Medical Society for Psychotherapy, editor of the Zentralblatt für Psychotherapie, and lecturer at the Federal Insti-tute of Technology in Zurich.[2] He also received a considerable number of honorary doctorates, the most notable of which were bestowed on him by Harvard and Oxford. And in 1938 while on a trip to India, he received additional doctorates from the Universities of Calcutta, Benares, and Allahbad.[3] Not sur-prisingly, it was during this period that Jung wrote the majority of his articles on Eastern religions, including pieces on yoga, Zen, and Tibetan Buddhism.[4]

By 1938 the political situation in Europe was in a steady state of deterioration which culminated in the beginning of World War II. Despite the threat of invasion, Jung remained in Switzerland during these years, writing a number of articles addressing the political and psychological situation in Germany.[5] This period in Jung's life came to a close in 1943 when he received the appointment of Professor of Medical Psychology at the University of Basel. Against this background of personal and historical events, we now turn to Jung's theoretical writings in which he attempted to elaborate the central ideas he had formulated during the formative phase of his life.

THE SECRET OF THE GOLDEN FLOWER

Jung first elaborated his ultimate concern in his 1929 commentary on *The Secret of the Golden Flower*, a Chinese Taoist text translated by Richard Whilhelm.[6] This book's importance lies in Jung's pioneering work on *mandala* symbolism; hereafter, the mandala would play a central role in Jung's thought. But before examining Jung's commentary, it may be helpful to note that Jung had drawn a number of mandalas as early as 1916, and in 1928, after reading Whilhelm's book, he came to realize that the mandala was a symbol of the self. Thus, for Jung, the mandala was the epitome of psychic wholeness and a symbol of his ultimate concern.

Furthermore, Jung found that the ideas in *The Secret of the Golden Flower* provided a foundation, if only a tentative one, which he could use to corroborate his own psychic discoveries. In the foreword to the second German edition of *The Secret of the Golden Flower*, Jung wrote:

> I had been investigating the processes of the collective unconscious since the year 1913, and had obtained results that seemed to me questionable in more than one respect. . . . My results based on fifteen years of effort, seemed inconclusive, because no possibility of comparison offered itself. I knew of no realm of human experience with which I might have backed up my findings with some degree of assurance. . . . The text that Wilhelm sent me helped me out of this difficulty.[7]

In psychological terms, Jung felt that the contents of his patients' dreams and fantasies were similar to the symbolism he found in this Chinese text, and that although the symbols differed in appearance, their underlying psychic structures (archetypes) were identical. Thus Jung used his archetypal theory to interpret the Chinese symbols, while using the Chinese symbolism to amplify his patients' dreams and fantasies. Most importantly, though, Jung interpreted the symbols he encountered in this text as expressing a psychic process leading to an experience of wholeness.

Jung felt that the pursuit of wholeness was essential for redressing the split between conscious and the unconscious.

Although the differentiation of consciousness from the unconscious is a natural part of psychic development, a total breach between the two realms can cause psychic problems. "The more powerful and independent consciousness becomes, and with it the conscious will, the more is the unconscious forced into the background. When this happens, it becomes easily possible for the conscious structure to be detached from the unconscious images."[8] The unconscious, however, does not succumb to repression, but instead reacts to the one-sided conscious orientation with an irruption of unconscious material.[9] The result of this conflict of opposites is a psychic civil war in which conscious and the unconscious are embroiled in an adversarial relationship.

It was in response to this psychic conflict that Jung sought a means to unify the psyche. "It is a question of yea-saying to oneself, of taking the self as the most serious of tasks, keeping conscious of everything done, and keeping it constantly before one's eyes in all its dubious aspects—truly a task that touches us to the core."[10] So, by paying careful attention to one's psychic contents, a unification of the psyche begins to take place.[11] In the Chinese world view the symbol of this unity is the Tao, which psychologically viewed represents "the beginning, in which everything is still unity, and which therefore appears as the highest goal. . . ."[12] The Tao or psychic wholeness is portrayed graphically by the mandala, a type of circular image enclosed in a square. Jung found that whenever this image appeared in the dreams and fantasies of his patients, it usually signified a return of psychic wholeness. Symbolically, Jung linked this unity with the mandala, and psychologically with the self, while in terms of the *Golden Flower*, he called this new center the "diamond body" or "indestructible body."[13] Psychically, the self acts as a new center of life, reconciling the fragmented components of the psyche into a harmonious whole. In this work, then, Jung specifically uses the terms unity, the Tao, the mandala, and the self as synonyms for his ultimate concern.

THE GOAL OF THERAPY

During the next few years Jung focused his attention on his lifelong interest in therapy and personality development. Broadly viewed, the stages of therapy were simply another way of speaking about the individuation process; the ultimate goal of both processes was the attainment of wholeness. In his 1929 article "Problems of Modern Psychotherapy," Jung divides the therapeutic process into four major components: confession, elucidation, education, and transformation.[14] In psychological language, the aim of confession is to bring to awareness anything that has been previously repressed from consciousness. This is an essential part of therapy since the repression of undesirable psychic contents leads to the formation of autonomous complexes, which in turn interfere with the workings of the conscious mind, acting as obstacles to the individuation process.

Repression is, moreover, antithetical to the ultimate goal of wholeness, since repressed contents—however undesirable they may be—are still part of the overall psychic structure and must be accepted as such. "I must have a dark side too if I am to be whole; and by becoming conscious of my shadow I remember once more that I am a human being like any other."[15] In this quote Jung uses the term *shadow* to refer to all those repressed contents of a personal nature. This preliminary reference to the shadow is destined to play a more decisive role in Jung's system, particularly in his alchemical writings. For now, though, the goal of the first stage of the therapeutic process is to shed light on the darkness of the shadow.

Despite shedding light on the shadow, deeper repressed contents, in the form of unresolved childhood emotions and dependency needs, still stand in the way of individual development. Generally, these contents are projected onto the analyst during the course of therapy. "That there should be a certain dependence on the doctor who has helped you is a perfectly normal and humanly understandable phenomenon. What is abnormal and unexpected is the extraordinary toughness of the tie and its imperviousness to conscious correction."[16] The stage of elucidation, then, is specifically designed to resolve this dependency so that the patient can gain a degree of autonomy; if successful, the patient comes to realize the "inescapable truth that to make claims on others is a childish self-indulgence which must be replaced by a greater sense of responsibility."[17]

Whereas Freud's psychoanalytic method is useful for elucidating the transference, Adler's method is helpful in educating the patient to social reality once the transference is resolved. That is to say, after the dissolution of the patient's childish illusions the patient is now ready to reenter society as a responsible citizen. "The patient must be drawn out of himself into other paths, which is the true meaning of 'education,' and this can only be achieved by an educated will."[18]

And finally, in the stage of transformation both doctor and patient are changed as they confront each other in the therapeutic process. This interaction evokes a fundamental transformation in the patient's basic personality structure, reaching far beyond adaptation to society. At this stage of therapy the doctor is no longer concerned simply with removing temporary barriers to adaptation or symptom reduction; rather, in Jung's view, the concern of the doctor is to address more fundamental life issues. By so doing, therapy "transcends its medical origins and ceases to be merely a method for treating the sick. It now treats the healthy or such as have a moral right to psychic health, whose sickness is . . . the suffering that torments us all."[19]

Here therapy concerns itself with the fundamental question of the meaning of life. As Jung observes, this is a crucial question, especially since many of his patients suffer from a sense of aimlessness and lack of meaning in their lives; in spite of affluence, social acceptance, and other external marks of success, something is still missing in their lives.[20] It is this deeper deficiency which Jung tries to address during the transformation stage of therapy. The cure for this problem, which provides life with ultimate meaning and value, is found in the symbols of the unconscious. In Jung's words: "It is only possible to live the fullest life when we are in harmony with these symbols; wisdom is a return to them."[21]

In a number of other articles written during this period, Jung explored further the themes of the meaninglessness of modern existence and psychology's role in responding to this crisis. In his 1931 essay "The Spiritual Problems of Modern Man," Jung makes two key observations: that the prevalance of meaninglessness in contemporary society has brought about an increased interest in psychology, and that the solution to the problem of meaninglessness is found in the psyche.[22] Jung addresses both of these points in the following quote. "The psychological interest of the present time is an indication that modern man expects something from the psyche which the outer world has not given him: doubtless something which our religion ought to contain, but no longer does contain, at least for modern man."[23] In particular, Jung saw his own system of thought as responding to the void created by the inability of traditional forms of religion to address the ultimate concerns of human existence.

Jung's view that the problem of meaninglessness is rooted in the psyche is clearly stated in another 1932 publication "Psychotherapists or the Clergy."[24]

> A psychoneurosis must be understood, ultimately, as the suffering of a soul which has not discovered its meaning. But all creativeness in the realm of the spirit as well as every psychic advance of man arises from the suffering of the soul, and the cause of the suffering is spiritual stagnation, or psychic sterility.[25]

In this quote Jung is no longer dealing with penultimate, therapeutic issues, but with questions that address the ultimate goal and purpose of life itself.[26] Not surprisingly, Jung views the problem of meaninglessness first and foremost as a psychic one; the deeper, underlying cause of meaninglessness is psychic fragmentation, which arises when the individual is cut off from the unconscious and its archetypal images.[27]

Since the problem of meaninglessness is a psychic one, so too is its solution. In response, Jung calls for a reawakening of the unconscious so that it can fertilize consciousness with its contents, and bring about a renewal of life.[28] Among other things, contact with the unconscious allows humans to experience a greater sense of selfhood and to find a new sense of meaning in life.

> The way of successive assimilation goes far beyond the curative results that specifically concern the doctor. It leads in the end to that distant goal which may perhaps have been the first urge to life: the complete actualization of the whole human being, that is, individuation.[29]

If meaninglessness is a symptom of psychic fragmentation, and wholeness is the cure, then the way to achieve this goal is to develop one's personality.

PERSONALITY DEVELOPMENT

In a November 1932 Vienna lecture published under the title "The Development of Personality," Jung once more takes up the issue of psychic growth. He sets the tone for the article by beginning with a quote from Goethe: "The Highest bliss on earth shall be the joys of personality."[30] The development of personality is a religious goal, as Jung makes clear when he writes that the "ultimate aim and strongest desire of all mankind is to develop that fullness of life which is called personality."[31] Personality development is also synonomous with the attainment of wholeness, and as such, is the antidote for humanity's discontent.[32] The goal of psychic development, and life itself, is to reconcile all psychic opposites, including the dark, repressed, shadow side of the personality, into a larger unity.

The development of the personality is, moreover, an innate drive which the therapeutic process, through a variety of means, seeks to nurture. This means wholeness is not something which occurs naturally, but must be cultivated in a formal way. Lest one think that the development of personality is something less than an ultimate goal, Jung makes it clear just how significant this goal is.

> The achievement of personality means nothing less than the optimum development of the whole individual being. . . . Personality is the supreme realization of the innate idiosyncrasy of a living being. It is an act of high courage flung in the face of life, the absolute affirmation of all that constitutes the individual, the most successful adaptation to the univeral conditions of existence coupled with the greatest possible freedom for self-determination.[33]

Jung quite obviously attributes an ultimate importance to the development of personality and the attainment of wholeness; indeed, it is Jung's response to the suffering and emptiness of life, for ultimately, only the "complete realization of our whole being" can bestow life with meaning.[34]

To further emphasize the significance of personality development, Jung speaks of it in religious terms, calling for "fidelity to the law of one's own being."[35] By this, he means that a person should trust in the inner laws of the psyche in much the same way that a "religious man" trusts in the will of God; but instead of God serving as the supreme authority, for Jung the ultimate authority is the psyche itself. Rather than follow a collective social mandate or the will of a transcendent being, Jung is proposing that one live in accordance with one's own innate psychic tendencies. Any thwarting of these tendencies in favor of external authority is antithetical to the quest for wholeness, which requires the inclusion of personal characteristics not always valued by the collective order.[36]

Jung argues, moreover, that the person who chooses to disregard social and religious conventions in deference to an individual path is "called" to this course of action by an inner necessity. Thus the quest for wholeness is a "vocation" that slowly, but inevitably, shapes the direction of one's life. Jung explicitly defines a vocation as "an irrational factor that destines a man to emancipate himself from the herd and from its well-worn paths. True personality is always a vocation and puts its trust in it as in God. . . . Anyone with a vocation hears the voice of the inner man: he is called."[37] Since the ultimate authority of life lies within the individual, there is nothing more important in life than to develop the innate tendency of the psyche to realize its wholeness. The psyche demands to be developed and to be made whole; obedience to this command is the highest good and the ultimate concern of life.[38]

But fidelity to the self-realization process does not mean a denial of the universal nature of human existence. Jung maintains that each person possesses a blueprint for development unique to the particular individual, and that despite differences in each blueprint, the final goal for all humans is the attainment of wholeness. Jung is attempting here to reconcile the universal and individual features of a human being: on the one hand, there are certain basic psychic structures that all human beings share in common, while on the other hand, there is something

distinctive about the way these universal features are manifest
in a given individual.

> So although the objective psyche can only be conceived as a
> universal and uniform datum, which means that all men share
> the same primary, psychic condition, this objective psyche
> must nevertheless individuate itself if it is to become actual-
> ized, for there is no other way in which it could express itself
> except through the individual human being.[39]

For Jung, therefore, human existence is simultaneously universal and particular, or stated otherwise, the following of the
universal inner laws of the psyche allows one to actualize those
qualities unique to the individual. Paradoxically, though, it is
by becoming an individual that "he will discover his identity
with the whole of humanity, as it ever was, is, and ever shall
be."[40] This statement points to an expansion of the psyche beyond
individual bounds to include a oneness of the individual with
all of humanity. "In some way or other we are part of a single,
all-embracing psyche, a single 'greatest man', the *homo maximus*,
to quote Swedenborg."[41]

The move from individual wholeness to cosmic unity was
a natural step for Jung given his interest in various forms of
Eastern philosophy. Indeed, he would have much more to say
about the oneness of the micro- and macrocosm in his alchemical
writings. For the moment, though, I simply want to emphasize
the importance Jung attributed to the quest for wholeness. The
pursuit of this goal is an ultimate concern which leads to the
complete fulfillment of one's human existence.

> The undiscovered vein within us is a living part of the psyche;
> classical Chinese philosophy names this interior way "Tao,"
> and likens it to a flow of water that moves irresistibly towards
> its goal. To rest in Tao means fulfillment, wholeness, one's
> destination reached, one's mission done; the beginning, end
> and perfect realization of the meaning of existence innate in
> all things. Personality is Tao.[42]

Between the years 1932 and 1934 Jung lectured and wrote on
a wide range of subjects, including articles on art, literature,

and modern civilization. In addition, in his 1934 article "A Study in the Process of Individuation," he continued to elaborate his ultimate concern. Originally published in *The Integration of the Personality*, the article was revised and later published in volume nine of the *Collected Works*.[43] My discussion is based on the earlier version. The significance of this article lies in Jung's integration of a number of themes from the previous few years, particularly his work on therapy and Eastern thought. For Jung, just as the Tao is a symbol of wholeness and a synonym for the self, so too the mandala symbolizes the Tao, wholeness, and self-realization. In this article Jung applies these theoretical formulations to a clinical study of one of his patients.[44]

The patient, a fifty-five-year-old, highly educated American woman who had come to Zurich to study and undergo analysis, had drawn a series of mandala-like paintings, the contents of which Jung analyzed. Through her analysis with Jung, the woman came to a number of insights concerning her various personal problems. But more importantly, the woman's development provided Jung with the opportunity to elaborate further the stages of psychic growth. The woman's first realization led her to an acceptance of the dark, evil, repressed side of her personality, the shadow, followed by an acceptance of the intellectual principle within the psyche, a reference to the animus of the woman, which needs to be developed as a counterbalance to the active Eros principle. Finally, and most importantly, a turning point occurred when the woman produced an image of a circle with a gold center, a symbol of the self. At that moment, she realized that the self, not the ego, is the center of the psyche. "She seized upon the important truth that the ego is not the centre of psychic life; that it revolves around the self, the centre, like a planet around the sun; and that this is consonant with universal laws."[45] In Jung's view, the self serves as both the starting and ending point of the entire process of psychic development; as the starting point it exists in a state of potentiality, while as the end point its realization signifies a realignment of the psychic structure.

Although a brief work, this article is important as a link in the elaboration of Jung's pattern of ultimacy, outlining as it does the stages of psychic development. Noticeably absent from his description of the individuation process is any mention of the persona, which played such a central role during the formative years. In its place, Jung emphasizes the confrontation with the shadow as the first stage of the individuation process. Likewise the mana figure, although not omitted, is relegated to a minor role. These changes indicate a modification in Jung's understanding of the individuation process.

In 1935 Jung wrote two articles, neither of which adds anything new to his ultimate concern; rather, they appear as attempts to consolidate the gains he had made in the previous few years. But for the purposes of historical integrity I will briefly describe their contents. The first of these articles "Archetypes of the Unconscious" is a summary of Jung's views on the collective unconscious. In that work he maintains a clear distinction between a personal and collective layer of the psyche, reiterates the ultimate importance of psychic development, and describes the stages of that process.[46] By this time Jung appears to have settled on a basic pattern of psychic development consisting of the shadow, anima/animus, and the self. There is nothing surprisingly new in his description of these figures at this time.

The other 1935 publication "The Tavistock Lectures" is based on a series of talks Jung gave at the Institute of Medical Psychology in London in which he attempted a grand synthesis of his work.[47] Lecture one is a review of his typological theory, while the second lecture addresses his understanding of the unconscious. Interestingly, in the third lecture, Jung turns to a discussion of his "complex theory." With Jung's increasing interest in the archetypes and the collective unconscious, his "complex theory" has diminished in importance, based as it is on the contents of the personal unconscious. Lecture four is concerned with dream interpretation, symbolism, and mythology, while the fifth lecture concludes with Jung's views on the transference phenomenon. Although not containing anything new, these lectures are an attempt by Jung to consolidate and further clarify his thought.

THE MANDALA

In a 1936 article "Dream Symbols of the Process of Individuation," Jung once again turned his attention to the mandala to elaborate his ultimate concern.[48] The basis of his discussion is his analysis of four hundred dreams taken from one of his patients. Three hundred fifty-five of the dreams, however, took place prior to Jung's personal contact with the patient, occurring while the patient was under the direct care of one of Jung's assistants. In his analysis of these dreams, Jung focuses on the ultimate goal of the individuation process — namely, the realization of the self and the attainment of wholeness.

> Symbols of the process of individuation are images, usually of archetypal nature, that appear in dreams and portray the centralizing process, or the production of a new centre of the personality. . . . I call this centre also the self, a term that is meant to include the totality of the psyche in so far as this manifests itself in an individual.[49]

Since the self is an archetype, it is known only through its images, particularly the image of the mandala. Jung, moreover, envisions the quest for wholeness as a process of transformation, beginning with the psyche in a state of fragmentation, and ending with its eventual unification. "Natural man is no *self*, but a particle of a mass, and even a mass, an aggregate, to such a degree that he is not even sure of his 'I'."[50] But through the process of individuation, the psyche is unified, and one's life is transformed; the symbol of this new, unified state of being is the mandala.

Jung mentions that the most important part of the mandala is the center, where traditionally a religious figure such as the Buddha or some other significant figure or image is located. Similarly, in Jung's view, the center of his patients' mandalas are also of ultimate importance, symbolizing as they do, the center of the psyche. "Hence the centre of the circle [mandala] as an expression of wholeness would correspond not to the 'I', but the self as epitome of the total personality."[51] But more than simply unifying one's psyche the bounds of the self extend beyond the individual to include a oneness with the world at large. The self, although expanded to cosmic proportions, is nonetheless located within a particular individual. Hence it is through the individual that one gains access to the universal. Using the language of the Upanisads, Jung writes that "the self is first of all the *personal atman*, but the latter is also the *superpersonal atman* with cosmic and metaphysical qualities."[52] In Jung's view, then, the psyche and the world form an inseparable unity rather than an irreconcilable duality. His thoughts on the nature of this unity are in a preliminary form, heavily influenced by the philosophies of the East and still awaiting their full elaboration in his alchemical writings.

Jung continued his investigation of the mandala as a unifying symbol in his well-known work *Psychology and Religion*.[53] The contents of this work are based on The Terry Lectures which Jung delivered in 1937 at Yale University. Primarily concerned with his understanding of religious phenomena, Jung also addresses the issue of wholeness, particularly in the third section of the work, "The History and Psychology of a Natural Symbol."[54]

Jung's discussion is based on an analysis of a number of mandalas taken from the dreams of one of his patients. What strikes Jung most about the mandalas is that the center, traditionally the seat of a sacred figure, is, in these cases, void of any such images.[55] In fact, Jung claims that as a rule, most of the mandalas produced by his patients do not contain religious figures in the center; rather, in place of the deity Jung found such objects as a star, flower, precious stone, or human being.[56] Historically speaking, this fact puzzled Jung, since the center is ordinarily the place of the deity. He reasoned that these objects must have a religious significance because, traditionally, the center is the place of the highest symbol, whatever form it takes. He concluded, therefore, that the center of his patients' mandalas were likewise of ultimate importance or of religious significance.[57]

When Jung questioned his patients about the meaning of the objects that occupied the place of the deity, most answered that the mandala had given them a sense of well-being and harmony. Jung summarizes his patients' reactions as follows:

"They came to themselves, they could accept themselves, they were able to become reconciled to themselves and by this they were also reconciled to adverse circumstances and events."[58] The appearance of the mandala signaled a new psychic condition qualitatively different from the previous one. Since the mandala symbolizes the self, Jung assumed that this new condition was one in which the fragmented psyche had been unified.

Specifically, with respect to the center of the mandala, he argues that "the place of the deity seems to be taken by the wholeness of man."[59] That is to say, psychic wholeness now assumes a position of ultimate importance. But rather than symbolizing a transcendent form of ultimacy, the mandala is a symbol for a nontranscendent form of psychological ultimacy. As Jung explains, the elevation of psychic wholeness to a level of ultimacy occurs when the energy previously invested in an external deity is withdrawn, and returned to its source in the psyche. Consequently, this withdrawal of projections results in a revitalization of the psyche. "But if the historical process of the despiritualization of the world—the withdrawal of projections—is going on as hitherto, then everything of a divine or demonic character must return to the soul to the inside of the unknown man."[60]

This means, then, that for those people who are no longer able to find meaning in an external deity, the center of the mandala becomes a symbol of religious significance.[61] Accordingly, the appearance of the mandala in dreams, for example, indicates an inward turning of attention until a deeper source of meaning is established in the unconscious. The mandala, in this respect, serves to focus psychic energy upon the self, thereby facilitating the withdrawl of energy from the external world. "Thus the mandala denotes and supports an exclusive concentration upon oneself. ... The circle, in this case, protects or isolates an inward process that should not become mixed with things outside."[62]

The ultimate goal of this process of interiorization is the realization of the self, and the attainment of psychic wholeness. But rather than focusing on the limited, personal ego, concentration on the self leads to an expansion of one's psychic horizons, for it is through the self that one gains access to that which is common to all of humanity. So, whereas the self is a psychological expression of wholeness, the mandala is its visual representation, symbolizing the "complete man."[63] In the final analysis, then, this makes the mandala a symbol of Jung's ultimate concern.

In his 1939 article "Conscious, Unconscious and Individuation" Jung gives a brief overview of the individuation process and its importance.[64] He reiterates that the goal of individuation is the attainment of wholeness: "I use the term 'individuation' to denote the process by which a person becomes a psychological 'individual', that is, a separate, indivisible unity, or 'whole'."[65] By wholeness, Jung affirms that he means more than simply ego-consciousness, but a larger psychic totality consisting of conscious and the unconscious. The process of individuation, therefore, requires a forging of these two seemingly irreconcilable halves into a larger psychic unity.

This reconciliation, however, is not based on a domination of either side of the psyche over the other, nor is it achieved by a blurring of the boundaries between the two sides. Rather, wholeness is achieved through a process of mutual yet conflicted interaction, based on the autonomy of each position. Although at times a painful process, conflict and confusion are, according to Jung, unavoidable parts of individuation. When successful, a new synthesis is forged from this clash between conscious and the unconscious. But the successful attainment of such a synthesis requires a total personal involvement in the process of psychic development; indeed, the commitment must be such that it is nothing short of an ultimate concern. "The attainment of wholeness requires one to stake one's whole being. Nothing less will do; there can be no easier conditions, no substitutes, no compromises."[66] Clearly the quest for wholeness must be approached as a religious goal around which the totality of one's existence revolves. In this way, the quest begins to encompasse more and more of one's life, until the ultimate goal, the unity of opposites is reached.

THE "CHILD" ARCHETYPE

Jung's 1940 essay "The Psychology of the Child Archetype" provides a further symbolic elaboration of wholeness.[67]

In this essay he distinguishes the psychic image of the child from the structure (archetype) which gives rise to it. In particular, the archetype of the "child god," according to Jung, appears throughout history in many different forms, the details of which need not concern us here. What is important, however, is the meaning of this archetype within the context of the individuation process.

Psychologically speaking, although the child archetype points to the "original" unconscious state of the psyche prior to the development of ego-consciousness, it also indicates the present condition of the psyche and compensates any imbalance in the conscious attitude.[68] In Jung's view, these two orientations (past and present) are related in the following way: as consciousness becomes more and more differentiated, it begins to move away from the unconscious and its rootedness in the archetypal past. Once the two realms are completely severed, life becomes empty and rootless, a meaningless fragment disconnected from a larger psychic/historical context, leaving one alienated from oneself and from the world at large. To compensate for this present psychic condition, the appearance of the child image in a dream, for example, is an attempt by the unconscious to reconnect the severed link with consciousness.

In addition to its past and present significance, the child archetype has a futuristic meaning, indicating psychic potentiality and the onset of imminent changes in the personality structure. Viewed within the context of the individuation process, Jung tells us that the "child" is a symbol of wholeness. "In the individuation process, it [the child] anticipates the figure that comes from the synthesis of conscious and unconscious elements in the personality. It is therefore a symbol which unites the opposites; a mediator, bringer of healing, that is, one who makes whole."[69] But note: when the child appears in multiple forms, its presence indicates a condition of psychic fragmentation, prior to the complete realization of wholeness—in that case it acts as an anticipatory figure.

On still other occasions the child appears in dreams and mythology as having a miraculous or difficult birth, images symbolizing the difficulty of giving birth to the self. "The motifs of insignificance, exposure, abandonment, danger, etc. try to show how precarious is the psychic possibility of wholeness, that is, the enormous difficulties to be met with in attaining this 'highest good'."[70] The individuation process can be thought of as a "rite of passage" in which the opposites of conscious and the unconscious collide and struggle with one another in an attempt to give birth to psychic wholeness. The psychological "child" of this process, the "highest good," the ultimate attainment of human existence, is the self. The self is born out of the conflict of opposites, reconciling the psyche into a new and harmonious whole. The "child" as an image of wholeness, is born from the "womb" of the unconscious, beginning as a seed, until it matures into a fully realized state of wholeness. Jung views this urge to wholeness as a "law of nature, of invincible power, even though its effect at the start is insignificant and improbable."[71]

For Jung, the self is the psychological equivalent of the Upanisadic conception of the *Atman*, which is both the center of the individual and the cosmos itself.

> The size and invincibility of the "child" are bound up in Hindu speculation with the nature of the atman, which corresponds to the "smaller than small yet bigger than big" motif. As an individual phenomenon, the self is "smaller than small"; as the equivalent of the cosmos, it is "bigger than big."[72]

Thus Jung's understanding of the self includes the oneness of the cosmos and the individual. More precisely, Jung believes that at the farthest reaches of the psyche, its individuality merges into the materiality of the world.[73] At some point the boundary between psyche and world blurs to the point of extinction so that rather than an impenetrable wall separating psyche and world, psyche and world appear as points on a continuum, forming an indivisible whole. In this sense, the child image, like the mandala and the Tao, becomes a symbol of a larger psyche/world unity.[74] Jung would now turn to alchemy for further symbolic material to elaborate his quest for wholeness.

Chapter Seven

Alchemy and Wholeness

Jung continued to elaborate his thought during the last phase of his life, which began in 1944 and ended with his death in 1961. The year 1944 was especially significant for Jung in that he nearly died from a heart ailment. Jung's health problems began on 11 February 1944 when he was hospitalized for treatment of a broken fibula after slipping on some ice. Ten days after his admittance, the heart trouble began, leaving Jung on the verge of death.[1] Jung reports in his autobiography of how, in a state of unconsciousness, he experienced "deliriums and visions" of being "high up in space" and seeing the earth below.[2] A dark block of stone then entered his vision. He approached the stone and attempted to enter it. At that moment he felt as if his entire earthly existence was stripped away from him and he experienced a sense of completeness and comfort in all that he had accomplished with his life. "This experience gave me a feeling of extreme poverty, but at the same time of great fullness. There was no longer anything I wanted or desired. I existed in an objective form; I was what I had been and lived."[3]

As Jung moved closer to the stone, he sensed that he would receive answers to many of his questions about life and "would meet the people who knew the answer to my question about what had been before and what would come after."[4] Jung's attention was then diverted to an image of his doctor, who approached him with a message stating that he must return to his earthly existence.[5] This disappointed Jung, since he wanted to enter the stone and receive the answers that awaited him. Although he slowly began to recover, his dreams and visions continued. In these dreams and visions, he felt himself at one with the universe, protected and safe in its embrace. "I felt as though I were floating in space, as though I were safe in the womb of the universe—in a tremendous void, but filled with the highest possible feeling of happiness."[6] This experience represented for Jung the ultimate unity, the *mysterium coniunctionis* he had been seeking all these years.[7] Eventually, though, the visions subsided, Jung's health improved, and he returned with renewed intensity to his work. In fact, this was the period of his life when all his major works on alchemy were written.

By 1947, although many students were now coming to Zurich to learn firsthand about Jung's work, there was no organizational structure available to accommodate the interest and needs of these students. To meet this need, Jung finally consented to the formation of the C.G. Jung Institute in Zurich, which offically opened 24 April 1948. Two years later Jung retired from the presidency, turning the institute affairs over to his close disciples. In addition to the training of analysts, the institute publishes research related to Jung's work and houses Jung's unpublished seminars and lectures.[8]

In 1955, on his eightieth birthday, Jung was honored at the meeting of the International Congress of Psychiatry held in Zurich. But tragedy also struck that year, as his wife of fifty-two years, Emma, died 30 November 1955. Despite the profound impact this loss had on Jung, he diligently continued his work. On his eighty-fifth birthday Jung was honored by the town of Küsnacht. By this time all his major works were completed, allowing him to concentrate on his autobiography and his final article written for the book *Man and His Symbols*.[9] Three weeks prior to his death, Jung suffered a slight stroke, forcing him to spend the last week of his life in bed, but still fully conscious. Jung's biographer, Barbara Hannah, describes a dream he reported having a few nights before his death. "He saw a big, round block of stone in a high bare place and on it was inscribed: 'This shall be a sign unto you of wholeness and oneness.' "[10]
Jung died shortly thereafter in his home at Kusnacht on 6 June 1961. The ashes of his cremated body are buried in Küsnacht next to the remains of his parents and wife. We now turn to a

discussion of Jung's alchemical writings during the last phase (1944-1961) of his life.

PSYCHOLOGY AND ALCHEMY

Whereas the elaboration of Jung's ultimate concern during the previous years (1929-1943) relied, in large part, on Eastern thought, Jung now relied on alchemy for additional symbolic material to amplify his thought.[11] Jung's interest in alchemy can be traced back to the commentary he wrote for Richard Whilhelm's *The Secret of the Golden Flower*. "Light on the nature of alchemy began to come to me only after I had read the text of the *Golden Flower*, that specimen of Chinese alchemy which Richard Wilhelm sent me in 1928. I was stirred by the desire to become more closely acquainted with the alchemical texts."[12]

In response to his interest in alchemy, Jung commissioned a Munich bookseller to acquire as many books as he could on the subject. After receiving the first such book and finding it incomprehensible, he let it sit untouched for nearly two years before returning to it. He then spent the next twenty-five years studying and writing about alchemy.

An understanding of Jung's writings on alchemy is important because he felt that the alchemical symbolism mirrored his own psychic discoveries.

> I had very soon seen that analytical psychology coincided in a most curious way with alchemy. The experience of the alchemists were, in a sense, my experience, and their world was my world. This was, of course, a momentous discovery: I had stumbled upon the historical counterpart of my psychology of the unconscious.[13]

Jung made the first substantial presentation of his findings in 1935 at the Eranos Congress where he referred to alchemical symbolism in his analysis of a series of dreams.[14] These lectures were later revised and appeared in their final form as parts two and three of *Psychology and Alchemy*.[15] This was followed by the 1937 publication of the abstracts of two lectures on alchemy given at the Zurich Psychological Club[16], which, in their pre-

liminary form, served as a starting point for Jung's 1946 publication on the relationship of alchemical symbolism to the
transference phenomenon.[17] Jung then gave a number of lectures on the Swiss alchemist, Paracelsus, in which he summarized the life and work of this legendary figure.[18] And finally, in
1942, Jung produced a longer, but still exploratory work on
Paracelsus and alchemy.[19]

Jung summarized his alchemical findings of the past few
years in his first major work on the subject, *Psychology and
Alchemy*; as such, this work serves as an excellent introduction
to Jung's more mature writings on the subject. In this work,
Jung claims that the alchemical symbolism depicts the psychic
contents of the alchemists, which they had unknowingly projected into matter. According to Jung, that which is unknown
(in this case matter) became a screen for the projection of unconscious contents.[20] Jung suggests that the alchemists' descriptions
have nothing to do with the properties of matter, but are descriptions of their own unconscious processes.

> I mean by this that while working on his chemical experi-
> ments the operator had certain psychic experiences which
> appeared to him as the particular behaviour of the chemical
> process. Since it was a question of projection, he was naturally
> unconscious of the fact that the experience had nothing to do
> with matter itself (that is, with matter as we know it today).
> He experienced his projection as a property of matter; but
> what he was in reality experiencing was his own unconscious.[21]

Consequently, Jung took the alchemists' description of the
stages of their work (*opus*) as depicting the adepts' own psychic
transformations; but more than simply a haphazard description
of psychic transformation, Jung felt that the alchemical symbolism, upon which he drew to elaborate his own quest for
wholeness, paralleled the stages of the individuation process.
He summarizes his position in another alchemical work from
this period.

> Anyone who attempted to describe the individuation process
> with the help of case-material would have to remain content
> with a mosaic of bits and pieces without beginning or end,

and if he wanted to be understood he would have to count on a reader whose experiences in the same field was equal to his own. Alchemy, therefore, has performed for me the great and invaluable service of providing material in which my experience could find sufficient room, and has thereby made it possible for me to describe the individuation process at least in its essential aspects.[22]

For Jung, the essence of the alchemical opus, as well as the individuation process, was aptly summarized by the alchemical motto of *solve et coagula* (dissolve and coagulate).[23] In alchemical terms, the alchemists saw their work as an attempt to form a unity out of the conflicting elements (earth, water, fire, and air) found in matter (the *prima materia*). And just as these conflicting elements were first separated in the alchemical *vas* before they were reunited into a harmonious whole, so too analysis begins with the analysand suffering from a "dissociation of the personality brought about by the conflict of incompatible psychic tendencies."[24] The goal of the individuation process, like that of alchemy, is the unity of all such opposites.

Here I need to mention that the material at the beginning of the alchemical opus is exactly the same as the finished product, although the material exists in a transformed state. Mythologically, the prima materia is symbolized by the figure Mercurius, whose presence resides over the entire work.[25] Although the work itself is concerned with the well-known idea of transforming lead into gold, strictly speaking the immediate goal of alchemy was the production of the *lapis philosophorum*, which, when applied to the lead, had the power to change it into gold. As we will see, the lapis, psychologically understood, is none other than the self.[26]

Generally speaking, Jung correlated his quest for wholeness with the alchemical stages of the *nigredo* or blackening stage, the *albedo* or whitening stage, and the *rubedo* or reddening stage.[27] Whereas during the nigredo the prima materia is treated until the hostile elements are separated, and the soul and spirit imprisioned in matter are released, during the albedo the vitalized soul/spirit pair is then rejoined to the dead material, animating it once again. And finally, during the rubedo, the reanimated body is returned to its primordial state of oneness in the form of the *Anthropos* or hermaphrodite, in which all opposites are reconciled.

ALCHEMY AND THE STAGES OF UNITY

After his introduction to the alchemical process in *Psychology and Alchemy*, Jung's first full-scale attempt to use the alchemical symbolism to elaborate his ultimate concern is found in his 1946 publication, *The Psychology of the Transference*.[28] By means of the alchemical imagery, Jung gives a detailed account of the stages leading to wholeness or in alchemical terms the *coniunctio*. "The idea of the *coniunctio* served on the one hand to shed light on the mystery of chemical combination, while on the other it became the symbol of the *unio mystica*, since, as a mythologem, it expresses the archetype of the union of opposites."[29]

Since the transference phenomenon, in the form of the projection of unconscious contents onto the analyst, results in the dissolution of the psyche into a chaotic state (*massa confusa*), psychic wholeness can only be attained when these projected contents are reclaimed and integrated into the larger psychic structure. In alchemical language, this state of unity is symbolized by the "royal marriage."[30] This entire process, beginning with the dissociation and projection of psychic contents and ending with their eventual unification, is still yet another version of the individuation process.[31]

Jung's analysis of the transference is based on a series of ten images found in a sixteenth-century alchemical text, the *Rosarium Philosophorum*. The first image depicts the mercurial fountain surrounded by four stars, symbolizing the presence of the four conflicting elements at the beginning of the work. Psychologically, it is a "pluralistic state of the man who has not yet attained inner unity, hence the state of bondage and disunion, of disintegration, and of being torn in different directions—an agonizing, unredeemed state which longs for union, reconciliation, redemption, healing and wholeness."[32] This is the beginning state of the individuation process, a state of conflict and fragmentation resulting from the projection of unconscious contents.

The second image portrays either a king and queen reaching out to one another in a gesture of marriage or a brother and sister pair in an incestuous embrace. In both cases the images symbolize the relationship between the psychic opposites of male (conscious) and female (unconscious). Psychologically, Jung views "incest" as an appropriate symbol of the individuation process and the union of opposites. "Incest symbolizes union with one's own being, it means individuation or becoming a self. . . . Incest is simply the union of like with like."[33] But before this union can occur, the residue of infantile emotions must be made conscious, so that they can later be integrated. This happens when they are projected onto the analyst; only then can the appropriate steps be taken to reclaim these projected psychic contents.[34] Here Jung views the work of the analyst as more than simply a therapeutic task.

> Small and invisible as this contribution may be, it is yet an *opus magnum*, for it is accomplished in a sphere but lately visited by the numen, where the whole weight of mankind's problems has settled. The ultimate questions of psychotherapy are not a private matter—they represent a supreme responsiblity.[35]

The sphere Jung is talking about is, of course, the psyche, upon which he bestows an ultimate importance. More exactly, the work of the psychotherapist becomes a "supreme responsibility" because it is a task whose goal is the development of the psyche and the attainment of wholeness.[36] Indeed, the quest for wholeness is not simply a penultimate issue; rather it is a matter of the highest concern for all of humanity.

The third image, which pictures a naked royal couple linked together by branches held in common and standing on an image of the sun and the moon, represents the opposites of Sol and Luna, or masculine and feminine. Psychologically, the naked couple indicates a condition of reality free of superficialities, a state in which "man stands forth as he really is and shows what was hidden under the mask of conventional adaptation: the shadow."[37] All the previously repressed "negative" contents are exposed in the course of therapy and slowly integrated into consciousness; if these contents are not brought to consciousness they are projected onto others. As Jung indicates, the reclamation of these repressed contents is a step toward wholeness, because one's dark, shadow side must be accepted as part of the overall psychic structure. Psychotherapy, rather than getting rid of one's shadow side, attempts to integrate these repressed contents so that one is no longer manipulated by them.[38] When these contents are integrated, "ego and shadow are no longer divided but are brought together in an—admittedly precarious—unity."[39] This is a preliminary form of unity but by no means the final coniunctio toward which the individuation process is moving.

The fourth image, depicting the king and queen sitting in a fountain filled with water, indicates a further step in the individuation process beyond the realm of the personal unconscious. It is a descent or immersion into the deeper layers of the unconscious, a return to a womblike condition in which consciousness is immersed in the collective unconscious. Here the masculine spirit and the feminine unconscious are in a state of potential wholeness awaiting their eventual rebirth. Therapeutically, this means one's projected fantasies are slowly starting to dissolve as they are subjected to analysis.

In the next image the sea has completely submerged the king and queen, who are now embraced in sexual intercourse. Their bodies have acquired wings, symbolizing their spiritlike nature, while the use of sexual imagery is symbolic of the coniunctio or union of opposites. "Our pictures of the *coniunctio* are to be understood in this sense: union on the biological level is a symbol of the *unio oppositorum* at its highest."[40] The descent into the unconscious depths is now complete; conscious and unconscious have returned to their initial state of unconscious identity.

The sixth image, showing the king and queen as one person with two heads, lying dead inside a tomb under the sea, symbolizes the next stage in the reconciliation of opposites. Psychologically, this is an intermediate state, or transitional condition in which the old psychic structure is obsolete but a new orientation has not yet arisen. "Since the *hermaphroditus* turns out to be the long-sought *rebis* or *lapis*, it symbolizes that mysterious being yet to be begotten, for whose sake the *opus* is undertaken. But the *opus* has not yet reached its goal, because the *lapis* has not come alive."[41] The death symbolism indicates an extinction of consciousness in the unconscious as well as a general stagnation of the psyche, prior to its renewal.

The unified male/female figure is a symbol of the union of the masculine consciousness with the feminine unconscious, indicating that just as the projected contents of the personal unconscious have to be integrated, so too must the projections emanating from the collective unconscious. The successful reclamation of these projected images gives birth to a new, enlarged psychic condition, which Jung calls the self. But rather than describing the self as a point midway between conscious and the unconscious, here the self — as the term for the union of all opposites — reaches out beyond the individual to the world at large. It is not that the psyche has been displaced as the locus of ultimacy but that the self has taken on cosmic dimensions.

> Reference must be made here to the Indian idea of the atman, whose personal and cosmic modes of being form an exact parallel to the psychological idea of the self. . . . The self too is both ego and non-ego, subjective and objective, individual and collective. It is the uniting symbol which epitomizes the total union of opposites.[42]

This unity, however, is still in a state of potentiality, since the dead king and queen must be reanimated if their unity is to have any basis in reality. In other words, the potential unity must be brought out of the unconscious into the light of conscious awareness.

Stage seven depicts the ascent of the king and queen to heaven, further symbolizing the potential state of wholeness "which has still to become a concrete fact."[43] But since one's former state of consciousness is no longer functional, one is left in a state of psychic chaos. Although the unconscious has been activated by the descent of consciousness, there is no ego to confront the contents arising from the unconscious. "This picture corresponds psychologically to a dark state of disorientation. The decomposition of the elements indicates dissociation and the collapse of the existing ego-consciousness."[44] In its descent into the unconscious, the ego's confrontation with the "non-ego" forces the ego to realize the relative nature of its own existence, which results in intense confusion and suffering. In order for the patient to withstand this confrontation with the unconscious and its contents, the therapist must seek to strengthen the patient's ego-consciousness by promoting critical understanding of the unconscious contents.

Whereas the previous stage represented the nigredo, with the stage of purification we move into the albedo. The albedo is the beginning of the reanimation of the king and queen, symbolized by the dew (spirit) falling on the deceased couple. The washing away of the darkness of the nigredo and its replacement by the light of the albedo represents the birth of a new perspective on one's psychic condition, arising, in part, from the critical examination of the unconscious contents. At this point one may even assume that this is the end goal of the process; but this is, in fact, not the case. Pure intellectual understanding is not sufficient to bring about the full realization of wholeness. "What is still lacking is heart or feeling, which imparts an abiding value to anything we have understood."[45] That is, one must not only acquire an objective intellectual understanding and "feeling-relationship" with the unconscious and its contents, but one must also gain an intuitive realization of one's wholeness, especially if it is to manifest itself as a living reality.[46]

During the ninth stage, although the soul is shown returning to the body and bringing it back to life, the reanimated body is quite different from what it was prior to its death; rather than two separate persons, the new body is now completely unified. Similarly, the structure of the psyche differs from its condition prior to analysis. Whereas before the descent of consciousness into the unconscious the personality revolved around the finite individual ego, after the "reanimation" of the psyche the universal self is the new center of the personality. "All these ideas lead one to conclude that not only the *coniunctio* but the reanimation of the 'body' is an altogether transmundane event, a process occurring in the psychic non-ego."[47] By transmundane Jung does not mean transcendent to the psyche, but rather that which is psychically beyond the bounds of the ego—namely, the self.

What is required at this stage, then, is the ability to discriminate what belongs to the personal ego from what belongs to the universal self. "The rational man, in order to live in this world has to make a distinction between 'himself' and what we might call the 'eternal man'."[48] The two realms must be discriminated between so that the ego is not subsumed by the unconscious. A strong ego is, moreover, essential for living in space/time reality, even though the ego is no longer the functioning center of the psyche. But despite its considerably deflated position in the psyche, the ego has gained new strength by virtue of its connection to the unconscious.

And finally we come to the last image, "the new birth," where the unified king and queen are fully resurrected. Here the hermaphrodite or Anthropos as a symbol of wholeness, manifests itself psychologically as the self. "The self wants to be made manifest in the work, and for this reason the *opus* is a process of individuation, a becoming of the self. The self is the total, timeless man and as such corresponds to the original, spherical, bisexual being. . . ."[49] At this stage one attains a unified state of being in which all projections are withdrawn and most psychic conflicts are resolved. But because the psyche is infinite in scope, the quest for wholeness remains an ongoing process. "The goal is important only as an idea; the essential thing is the *opus* which leads to the goal: *that* is the goal of a lifetime."[50] Nonetheless, a transformation has occurred that now places the self at the center of the personality, reconciling all opposites into a harmonious whole.

During 1946 Jung also published a foreword to a work on alchemy written by Ian MacPhail.[51] His publications in 1947, on the other hand, included four book forewords, none of which were concerned with alchemy.[52] In 1948 Jung wrote an introductory article on the spirit Mercurius based on two lectures he had given at the Eranos Conference in 1942.[53] Without going into unnecessary detail, a few remarks are in order. First, Mercurius is a symbol of both the beginning and end of the alchemical opus. As the initial state he is synonomous with the nigredo, while at the end he is known as the "uroboros, the One and All, symbolizing the union of opposites."[54] In his role as the reconcilor of opposites he is the psychological equivalent of the self. The ideas in this work, like most of Jung's previous writings on alchemy, would eventually find their way into *Mysterium Coniunctionis*.

But prior to completion of that work, during 1951 Jung published *Aion*, a book-length work on the symbolism of the self.[55] What is noteworthy for our purposes is Jung's use of Christ as a further symbolic amplification of the self. "These few, familiar references should be sufficient to make the psychological position of the Christ symbol quite clear. Christ exemplifies the archetype of the self."[56] By this time Jung had ascribed to the self the status of a "god-image," thus making Christ simply one of many possible manifestations of this image. The "god-image," like the self, is a psychological expression of wholeness, and is portrayed graphically by either a deity or a geometric figure such as a mandala.[57]

The self, then, as the archetype of wholeness, becomes the basis for the various expressions of the deity found in the monotheistic faiths. "Finally the self, on account of its empirical peculiarities, proves to be the eidos behind the supreme ideas of unity and totality that are inherent in all monotheistic and monistic systems."[58] Eventually Jung extended this claim to include all god images, not just those of the monotheistic religions. This position is in keeping with the ultimate importance he attributed to the psyche, wherein the psyche and its images, particularly the self, are primary, while any externalization of these images is viewed as a secondary phenomenon. Hence Jung portrays Christ as a symbol of the self rather than using the self as a symbol of Christ.[59]

After this excursion into Christian symbolism, Jung once again turned his attention to his alchemical researches.[60] In 1952 he wrote his "Introduction to the Religious and Psychological Problems of Alchemy," and in 1954 he wrote an article on the "Philosophical Tree," with particular attention to its significance in alchemy.[61] In another introductory work on alchemy written in 1954, "The Visions of Zosimos," Jung described the thought of this Greek alchemist.[62] All Jung's writings on alchemy, though, were leading to his final major work, *Mysterium Coniunctionis* which contains his final statements about alchemy as well as the individuation process.

MYSTERIUM CONIUNCTIONIS

Jung found in alchemy a rich source of symbolic material that he could use to amplify his ultimate concern and pattern of ultimacy. Like the individuation process, Jung felt that the goal of the alchemical procedure was the attainment of unity.

> Alchemy with its wealth of symbols, gives us insight into an endeavor of the human mind which could be compared with a religious rite, an *opus divinum*. The difference between them is that the alchemical *opus* was not a collective activity . . . but rather . . . an individual undertaking on which the adept staked his whole soul for the transcendental purpose of producing a unity.[63]

Hence, Jung appropriately subtitled his work "An Inquiry into the Separation and Synthesis of Psychic Opposites in Alchemy." The book itself is divided into six sections, of which the most important for our purposes is the last part on the coniunctio. The first five sections set the stage for the coniunctio, where Jung discusses the ultimate goal of psychic development.

In section one Jung describes the "components of the coniunctio," with special emphasis on the various pairs of opposites which later culminate in the coniunctio, including cold/warm, spirit/soul, male/female, living/dead, and a host of others.[64] Psychologically, "the pairs of opposites constitute the phenomenology of the paradoxical *self*, man's totality."[65] Section two is a further analysis of the paradoxical nature of the self, this time viewed in terms of the lapis philosophorum. The lapis functions as both the prima materia and end product of the work, and is described as both base and precious, and volatile and solid. Likewise these same paradoxes apply to the self which, psychologically speaking, is both the beginning and end of the individuation process.[66] In section three Jung interprets the alchemical opposites of Sol and Luna in psychological terms as consciousness (Sol) and the unconscious (Luna). The goal of both alchemy and individuation is the union of these opposites in the lapis or self. The next section is devoted to the alchemical symbolism of king and queen, which are also used to personify the paradoxical nature of the prima materia. In Jung's view, the king "personifies a hypertrophy of the ego which calls for compensation."[67] As might be expected the source of this compensation is the unconscious; but before the "sick king" (the ego) can be healed, he must first be dissolved into his basic components during the nigredo phase of the alchemical opus.[68]

In psychological language the dissolution of the king symbolizes the descent of the ego into the unconscious from where it initially arose. "For these reasons, too, the king constantly needs the renewal that begins with a descent into his own darkness, an immersion in his own depths, and with a reminder that he is related by blood to his adversary."[69] Although the adversary, in the form of the queen or anima figure, later becomes the source of the kings renewal, the initial contact with the unconscious is only a preliminary stage in the attainment of wholeness, a fleeting glance of what lies ahead. "Consciousness is no longer under the dominion of the unconscious, in which state the dominant is hidden in the darkness, but has now glimpsed and recognized a supreme goal."[70] The supreme goal is, of course, the attainment of wholeness, toward which the entire individuation process is moving. But this initial glimpse of wholeness also causes difficulty because the unconscious is now in open conflict with the ego. Previous to the ego's descent into the unconscious, and the activation of the unconscious, the ego assumed itself to be the sole ruler of the psyche, whereas now it realizes this is not the case. In psychotherapy this is a period of utter chaos, conflict, and darkness. By contrast to the alchemists who called this stage of their work the nigredo, Jung equates it with the confrontation with the shadow.[71] The ego has now descended into the dark, repressed layer of the psyche where all the material unacceptable to the ego is located. Despite the conflict, the king (ego) is on the verge of gaining entrance to the deeper collective unconscious, the source of his renewal.

Section five is concerned with the prima materia and more or less summarizes the previous stages of the work. It is, however, not until section six, the conjunction, that we reach the central part of both the alchemical opus and the individuation process. During this phase the potential state of wholeness is gradually raised out of the unconscious until it is fully and consciously realized. Alchemically, the final realization of wholeness consists of three parts: a mental union, a mind/body union, and mind/world unity.

The first union, or *unio mentalis*, consists of a separation and later reunion of the spirit and soul after their abstraction from matter (prima materia) during the nigredo. In psychological terms, one achieves the unio mentalis by intensive investigation of the unconscious and its contents.[72] Introspection and analysis thus provide an intellectual perspective on one's emotional and psychic condition, as well as knowledge about the operation and contents of the unconscious, particularly the shadow.

Alchemically, the union taking place during the albedo, consisting of the reuniting of the spirit/soul complex with the body, corresponds psychologically to the internalization of the insights gained from the intellectual analysis of the unconscious. Despite having gained various insights from the analysis of the unconscious, these insights now need to be made an integral part of one's daily existence. "The second stage of conjunction therefore consists in making a reality of the man who has acquired some knowledge of his paradoxical wholeness."[73] This is accomplished through actively engaging the images and moods of the anima, which, among other things, gives birth to a new, unified psychic center. This new center, the self, rather than simply a theoretical possibility, now becomes a living reality, acting as the guiding center of one's life.

And this brings us to the final union, the *unus mundus*, signifying the return of the unified body/soul/spirit to its initial oneness with the universe.[74] Jung, like the alchemists, views the previous two conjunctions as preliminary stages of the opus: "For us the representation of the idea of the self in actual and visible form is a mere *rite d'entree*, as it were a propaedeutic action and mere anticipation of its realization."[75] While it is true that the second union does bring about a degree of psychic wholeness, it is a wholeness that is still separate from the external world. It is not until the last stage, culminating in the unus mundus, that the unified psyche finally realizes its unity with all of existence. Jung, relying on the work of the alchemist Gerhard Dorn, gives the following description of the unus mundus. "The creation of unity by a magical procedure meant the possibility of effecting a union with the world—not with the world of multiplicity as we see it but with a potential world, the eternal Ground of all empirical being. . . ."[76] Jung also equates this condition with the unity of *yin* and *yang* in the Tao or "the experience of *satori* in Zen."[77] The unus mundus, psychologically understood, refers, therefore, to a totality in which psyche and world are unified, or in other words, a condition where the self embraces both psyche and world to form an indivisible totality.[78]

Jung uses the mandala to symbolize this cosmic unity. "The mandala symbolizes, by its central point, the ultimate unity of all archetypes as well as of the multiplicity of the phenomenal world, and is therefore the empirical equivalent of the metaphysical concept of the *unus mundus*."[79] In this statement Jung equates the mandala with the alchemical concept of the unus mundus. As we know, the mandala is a symbol of the self, while the self is what unifies the psyche; but not only does the self unify the psyche, it also functions as the meeting point of the psyche and world. It is this unity which forms the psychological equivalent of the unus mundus.[80]

To account for the unitary nature of psyche and world, Jung coined the term "psychoid unconscious." So, rather than positing an external metaphysical being or reality as the unifier of psyche and world, Jung roots the unity in the unconscious.

> In view of this extremely uncertain situation it seems to me very much more cautious and reasonable to take cognizance of the fact that there is not only a psychic but also a psychoid unconscious before presuming to pronounce metaphysical judgements which are incommensurable with human reason.[81]

More precisely, the "psychoid unconscious" can be considered a further gradation of the unconscious where self and world meet, and where all opposites are reconciled. In the final analysis, then, the nexus of the micro- and macrocosm is the individual.

Although Jung continued to work and publish a number of articles during the last five years of his life, there were no major changes in his thought. Clearly, his thought reached its climax with the publication of *Mysterium Coniunctionis*, as Jung himself indicates in his autobiography. "In *Mysterium Coniunctionis* my psychology was at last given its place in reality and established upon its historical foundations. Thus my task was finished, my work done, and now it can stand."[82]

SUMMARY

Throughout this period we have seen how Jung elaborated his ultimate concern and pattern of ultimacy. Initially, drawing heavily on Eastern thought, Jung used such ideas and images as the Tao, the mandala and the Atman to amplify his ultimate concern. These ideas provided a foundation for Jung's psychological concepts, particularly the idea of the self and its oneness with the universe. In addition to elaborating his ultimate concern there were various modifications in his pattern of ultimacy, the most notable being the omission of the persona and the inclusion of the shadow in the individuation process. Although the remainder of the stages of the individuation process remained intact, new symbolic material gathered from Jung's alchemical researches was used to amplify his thought. In short, then, during this period, Jung enriched and elaborated his ultimate concern and pattern of ultimacy. But despite the introduction of various modifications, there was no radical break with his previous formulations. The quest for wholeness remained as his ultimate concern and the individuation process served as the path leading to that goal.

Chapter Eight

Conclusion

At the beginning of this study I indicated the wide-ranging nature of Jung's writings. I also mentioned that there are a variety of ways to approach Jung's thought and that a particular approach sets the perimeters of one's study. A theological investigation of Jung's system, for example, is quite different from the approach of a literary critic, which is simply to say that one's interests determine the types of questions one asks of the data. Because I chose to approach Jung's thought from the perspective of the history of religions, my interest in this study centered on an examination of the religious goal or ultimate concern of his psychotherapeutic system. This interest required the asking of two questions: What was Jung's ultimate concern? and To what extent did it change over time?

The method used to answer these questions was descriptive not evaluative; rather than make normative judgements about the truth claims of Jung's system, my goal was to describe what Jung said and when he said it. Outside interpretive categories — whether theological or psychological, for example — were not introduced to evaluate his claims or to explain why Jung held a particular belief. Instead all statements were validated by the available historical data contained within Jung's system. The aim, therefore, was to understand Jung's religious goal and then to trace the evolution of that goal throughout his *Collected Works*.

But before the evolution of Jung's religious goal could be determined, it was necessary to arrange Jung's writings in historical sequence, since the editing of the *Collected Works* according to themes instead of chronology tends to mask the changes in his thought. Once the historical documentation was arranged chronologically, it was then possible to conceptualize the religious goal of Jung's system as the quest for wholeness. As we have seen, wholeness is synonomous with the reconciliation of opposites and is the normative goal of psychic development. Generally speaking, Jung envisioned wholeness as the ultimate level of human attainment; it is his ideal image of what it means to be a full human being.

Viewed in religious terms, the self-realization process can be understood as a nontranscendent form of psychological ultimacy. It is nontranscendent in that Jung avoids externalizing the psychological experience of the self as an external deity. Accordingly, his religious goal is psychological, since his ultimate concern is with the development of various psychic processes, most notably the realization of the self. Jung confers upon the self a religious significance, claiming, as he does, that the realization of the self is the "highest" and "ultimate purpose" of life. "The beginnings of our whole psychic life seem to be inextricably rooted in this point, and all our highest and ultimate purposes seem to be striving towards it."[1]

This means that Jung squarely places the burden of ultimate meaning on the human plane, bestowing upon the individual a pivotal role in the universe. "All life is individual life, in which alone the ultimate meaning is to be found."[2] At the same time, individual existence, although unique, is, however, not cut off from the rest of the universe but is an intricate part of a larger cosmic totality. Jung's concluding remarks in *Mysterium Coniunctionis* sum up the significance of human existence. "That a psychological approach to these matters draws man more into the centre of the picture as the measure of all things cannot be denied. But this gives him a significance which is not without justification."[3] What is ultimately important in the universe is not transcendent to human existence but is found in the depths of the human psyche; that is, with the realization of the self and the attainment of wholeness, the ultimate goal of life is reached. In this sense the quest for wholeness functions as more than a penultimate therapeutic concern; it is the religious goal of Jung's system. So, despite Jung's refusal to speculate on a variety of metaphysical questions, his thought is not neutral when it comes to the religious question of human ultimacy. But this is not a criticism. On the contrary, many people, including some of Jung's patients, were attracted to his thought precisely because it provided a comprehensive framework for understanding their place in the universe.

Thus, Jung's system, with its psychological analysis of the human condition and its wide range of techniques designed to transform it, functions as a religious path, especially for those people who are no longer able to find meaning in more traditional religious forms. Neither sin and redemption, nor ignorance and wisdom, but fragmentation and wholeness are the pairs of opposites forming the center of the religious quest. But this quest is more than a narcissistic pursuit of limited ego concerns, for to actualize the self is the point of entry into a larger cosmic totality. Naturally, it follows that, for Jung, the ultimate authority in life is not an external one—be it church or state—but an internal one. Only when the self becomes the new center of life is it possible to live a full and authentic existence, free of external demands. At that moment, external aspects of existence are no longer the measure of a person; what is unique and important is the inner world of the psyche.[4] By shifting the locus of ultimacy from the cosmos to the depths of the psyche Jung sanctified individual existence, bestowing upon human existence a central importance in the larger scheme of things. In this respect Jung's work serves as a bridge between the psychological and religious spheres of life.

We have also seen that the evolution of Jung's thought went through three distinct phases, which I have labelled "developmental," "formative," and "elaborative."[5] The central thread running through Jung's work during the developmental phase was the idea of psychic fragmentation; almost without fail, his writings were attempts to understand the fragmentation of the human psyche. While the key conceptual tools in his attempt to explain this fragmentation were the personal unconscious and the "complex," his method for investigating the psyche depended on empirical studies and the theories of Freud. Therapeutically, he was concerned with how complexes impinged on ego consciousness and how their effects could be lessened or alleviated.

These penultimate, therapeutic concerns dominated Jung's writings throughout most of this period.

During the formative phase Jung not only sought and found the means to unify the fragmentation of the psyche, but his interest in the unconscious shifted from the objective investigation of various mental disorders to an involvement with his own psychic processes. This marked the moment when his thought began its movement from a penultimate therapeutic concern to a religious concern addressing itself to the ultimate meaning and purpose of life.[6] Concomitant with this shift, the realization of the self appeared as his religious goal, and the individuation process as his pattern of ultimacy.[7] So, rather than simply addressing therapeutic issues in his theoretical writings as he had in the previous period, his statements about the psyche were now endowed with religious significance; that is, he viewed the realization of the self and the attainment of wholeness as the ultimate goal of life. Moreover, Jung's thought during this period underwent a shift from an ego-based personal psychology to a self-based archetypal psychology, in which the archetypes of the collective unconscious had gained prominence over the ego and the contents of the personal unconscious. But despite these modifications in his thought, the individual was still viewed as separate from the world at large.

The elaborative phase of Jung's life exhibits continuity with the previous one. Rather than a radical break in his ultimate concern, Jung modified and amplified his thought by extending it into a variety of cultural domains, the two most important being Eastern philosophy and alchemical symbolism. These systems provided Jung with a new theoretical basis for his work, as well as a ready source of material to elaborate his ultimate concern and pattern of ultimacy. In particular, Jung correlated the individuation process with the alchemical stages of the nigredo, albedo, and rubedo.[8] The nigredo, which corresponded to the ego's confrontation with the shadow as it descended into the unconscious, precipitated the beginnings of an intense crisis experience filled with suffering and uncertainty. So, whereas the crisis experience during the formative phase of Jung's work resulted from the persona's breakdown, here the confrontation with the shadow is the source of confusion. Consequently, during this time Jung viewed the ego as playing a more active role in the individuation process, descending as it does into the depths of the unconscious, rather than passively waiting for the unconscious to overwhelm it. Hence, the ego must first subject itself to extinction in the unconscious before the birth of the self can take place. According to Jung: "From this we can see the numinous power of the self, which can hardly be experienced in any other way. For this reason *the experience of the self is always a defeat for the ego.*"[9] In this statement, Jung specifically links up access to the numinous quality of the self with the "defeat of the ego." Only then is the self ready to assume its rightful place as the center of the psyche.

Once the wholeness latent in the unconscious is activated, it then has to be raised to consciousness, which marks the transition to the albedo and the establishment of a relationship with the anima. The anima serves as a conduit between conscious and the unconscious through which the archetypal images flow. Out of this interaction between consciousness and the unconscious, the self, as the new center of the personality, is born. Although the self consists of the reconciliation of all psychic opposites, it still remains separated from the outer world. As previously stated, this dualistic conception of psyche and world is the point where Jung's description of the individuation process ended during the formative phase.

By contrast, throughout the elaborative period, but most notably in *Mysterium Coniunctionis*, Jung speculated on a further stage of psychic development consisting of a unification of the psyche with the cosmos.[10] By so speculating, Jung's understanding of the self was expanded to cosmic proportions, serving as the unifier of psyche and world. Whereas his conception of psyche and world was dualistic during the formative phase, here his thought is clearly unitary. Furthermore, to account for this unified understanding of the psyche Jung introduced the concept of a psychoid unconscious. Although cosmic in nature, Jung nonetheless located the conjunction of the micro- and macrocosm in the individual, thus bestowing upon the individual a central role in the universe.

With this, we are now in a position to make a number of final observations about the evolution of Jung's ultimate concern. First, there is a direct line from his writings on the fragmentation of the psyche, leading to his search for psychic unity and ending in his alchemical speculations on the self/world unity. Corresponding to these changes there is also a shift in Jung's understanding of the unconscious. Whereas in the first phase the emphasis was on the personal unconscious and its contents, particularly the complexes, in the formative phase Jung sought and found in the self the means to unify the fragmented psyche. He also expanded his conception of the unconscious to include a collective layer. And finally, during the elaborative phase Jung enlarged his notion of the self to cosmic proportions so that the self became the linchpin between psyche and world. Thus, the evolution of Jung's religious goal exhibits a movement from psychic fragmentation, to individual wholeness, to cosmic unity. The quest for wholeness was the thread which provided continuity to Jung's thought and served as the ultimate concern of his psychotherapeutic system.

Notes

INTRODUCTION

1. The best example of this endeavor is found in Morton Kelsey, *Christo-Psychology* (New York: Crossroad Publishing Company, 1982).

2. For a good example of the application of Jung's thought in therapy see June Singer, *Boundaries of the Soul* (Garden City, New York: Doubleday Publishing, 1972), and Murray Stein ed., *Jungian Analysis* (Boulder: Shambhala, 1984). Examples of the use of Jung's theories to interpret literary works are Maud Bodkin, *Archetypal Patterns in Poetry* (London: Oxford University Press, 1934); Marie-Louise von Franz, *An Introduction to the Interpretation of Fairy-Tales* (New York: Spring Publications, 1970), and Barbara Hannah, *Striving towards Wholeness* (New York: G.P. Putnam's Sons, 1971).

3. Two works typical of this approach are Marie-Louise von Franz, trans. William Kennedy, *C.G. Jung: His Myth in Our Time* (New York: G.P. Putnam's Sons, 1975), and Gerhard Adler, "C. G. Jung' s Contribution to Modern Consciousness," *British Journal of Medical Psychology* 20 (1945): 207-220.

4. For a detailed account of the religio-historical method see Robert D. Baird, *Category Formation and the History of Religions* (The Hague: Mouton, 1971). A description of this method will be given later in this work.

5. Ibid., 25.

6. Speaking in more general terms, the psychologist of religion Don

Browning has argued that the modern psychologies "are, in fact, mixed disciplines which contain examples of religious, ethical, and scientific languages." Don S. Browning, *Religious Thought and the Modern Psychologies* (Philadelphia: Fortress Press, 1987), 8. Although Browning extends his observation to Jung's thought, he does not undertake a historical analysis of Jung's religious goal. Unfortunately, since the present study was already completed when Browning's work appeared, I was not able to incorporate fully his findings at this time.

CHAPTER 1. APPROACH TO JUNG

1. A thorough bibliographic source that includes articles, books, and dissertations is found in Joseph Vincie and Margreta Rathbauer-Vincie, *C.G. Jung and Analytical Psychology: A Comprehensive Bibliography* (New York: Garland Publishing, 1977). This work contains almost four thousand entries written between the years 1900 and 1976. An extensive computer search was used to check on sources from 1976 to the present.

2. The two main sources for this biographical review are C.G. Jung, *Memories, Dreams, Reflections*, ed. Aniela Jaffe (New York: Vintage Books, 1965), and Henri F. Ellenberger, *The Discovery of the Unconscious* (New York: Basic Books, 1970).

3. Jung, *Memories, Dreams, Reflections*, 91.

4. Ibid., 80.

5. Ibid., 56.

6. Jung's dissertation was originally published in German as, *Zur Psychologie und Pathologie sogenannter occulter Phänomene* (Leipzig: Oswald Mutze, 1902).

7. Jung, *Memories, Dreams, Reflections*, 108-109.

8. While it is true that Jung mentioned that the discovery of psychiatry served as the point where his biological and spiritual interests merged, there is nothing in his *Collected Works* to suggest the presence of an ultimate concern, at least on the ideal level at this period. See Jung, *Memories, Dreams, Reflections*, page 109 for a description of this event.

9. C.G. Jung, *The Collected Works of C.G. Jung,* (hereafter C.W.) 20 vols., ed., Sir Herbert Read, Michael Fordham, Gerhard Adler, trans. R.F.C. Hull, Bollingen Series XX, (Princeton: Princeton University Press, 1953-1979). Vol. 2, *Experimental Researches,* trans., Leopold Stein.

10. William McGuire, ed. trans. Ralph Manheim and R.F.C. Hull, *The Freud/Jung Letters* (Princeton: Princeton University Press, 1974).

11. This work is now part of C.W. 3, *The Psychogenesis of Mental Disease.*

12. The 1912 German title of this work was, *Wandlungen und Symbole der Libido* (Leipzig and Vienna: Franz Deuticke, 1912). For the English version, see *Psychology of the Unconscious* (New York: Moffat, Yard, 1916).

13. C.G. Jung, C. W. 6, *Psychological Types.*

14. C.G. Jung, C.W. 14, *Mysterium Coniunctionis.*

15. C.G. Jung, "Approaching the Unconscious," in *Man and His Symbols,* ed., Carl G. Jung (New York: Dell Publishing, 1964), 1.

16. Barbara Hannah, *Jung: His Life and Work* (New York: G.P. Putnam's Sons, 1976).

17. Ibid., Preface.

18. I have already mentioned von Franz, *C. G. Jung: His Myth in Our Time.* For another example see Laurens Van der Post, *Jung and the Story of Our Time* (New York: Random House, 1977).

19. Paul Stern, *C.G. Jung: The Haunted Prophet* (New York: George Braziller, Inc., 1976).

20. Ibid., 256.

21. Among the better biographies presently available are those by Vincent Broom, *Jung* (New York: Atheneum, 1978), and Ellenberger, *The Discovery of the Unconscious,* 657-748.

22. Morton Kelsey, *Christo-Psychology,* xi.

23. John P. Dourley, *The Illness That We Are: A Jungian Critique of Christianity* (Toronto: Inner City Books, 1984), and Wallace B. Clift, *Jung and Christianity: The Challenge of Reconciliation* (New York: Crossroad, 1982).

24. Gerald G. May, *Will & Spirit: A Contemplative Psychology* (New York: Harper & Row, 1982), 293.

25. Harold Coward, *Jung and Eastern Thought* (Albany: State University of New York Press, 1985).

26. Ibid., 3-28, and 29-60.

27. Nathan Katz ed., *Buddhist and Western Psychology* (Boulder: Prajna Press, 1983), 241-262.

28. David Cox, *Jung and Saint Paul* (New York: Association Press, 1959); John Welch, *Spiritual Pilgrims: Carl Jung and Teresa of Avila* (New York: Paulist Press, 1982), and John Dourley, *The Psyche as Sacrament: C.G. Jung and Paul Tillich* (Toronto: Inner City Books, 1981).

29. Philip Rieff, *The Triumph of the Therapeutic* (New York: Harper & Row, 1966), 139.

30. May, 294.

31. This is an example of what Baird has called the "essential-intuitional" method, whereby one intuits the essence of religion and then proceeds to judge what is and is not religion based on one's intuition. For a full discussion see Robert D. Baird, *Category Formation and the History of Religions* 2-5. A summary of Baird's position will be presented later in this chapter.

32. May, 10.

33. James Heisig, *Imago Dei: A Study of C. G. Jung's Psychology of Religion* (London: Associated University Presses, 1979).

34. C.G. Jung, C.W. 11, *Psychology and Religion: West and East*.

35. Aubrey Lewis, "Jung's Early Work," *The Journal of Analytical Psychology* 11 (July 1957): 119-136.

36. Kenneth Lambert, "Jung's Later Work," *Journal of the American Psychoanalytic Association* X (January 1962): 191-197, and Aniela Jaffe, *Jung's Last Years* (Dallas: Spring Publications, 1984). In particular see chapter V, "The Creative Phases in Jung's Life." See also Michael Fordham, "The Evolution of Jung's Researches," *British Journal of Medical Psychology* 29 (1956): 3-8.

37. Calvin Hall and Vernon Nordby, *A Primer of Jungian Psychology* (New York: Mentor, 1973); Anthony Storr, *C.G. Jung* (New York: Viking Press, 1973), and Edward C. Whitmont, *The Symbolic Quest* (Princeton: Princeton University Press, 1969).

38. Jolande Jacobi, *Der Weg zur Individuation* (Zurich: Rascher, 1965).

39. Edward Edinger, *Ego and Archetype: Individuation and the Religious Function of the Psyche* (New York: Penguin Books, 1972), and Josef Goldbrunner, *Individuation* (Notre Dame: University of Notre Dame Press, 1964). See also, Marie-Louise von Franz, "The Process of Individuation," in *Man and His Symbols*, ed. Carl G. Jung (New York: Dell Publishing, 1964), 157-254.

40. Ellenberger, 657-748.

41. Peter Homans, *Jung in Context* (Chicago: The University of Chicago Press, 1979).

42. Ibid., 21.

43. Ibid., 26.

44. In particular I am thinking of vol. 7 of the C.W., *Two Essays on Analytical Psychology*, and vol. 14, *Mysterium Coniunctionis*.

45. For Jung's alchemical writings see the following volumes in the C.W.: vol. 12, *Psychology and Alchemy*, vol. 13, *Alchemical Studies*, and vol. 14, *Mysterium Coniunctionis*.

46. Mary Ann Mattoon, *Jungian Psychology in Perspective* (New York: The Free Press, 1981), 186-188.

47. James Hillman, "The Great Mother, Her Son, Her Hero, and the Puer," from *Fathers and Mothers: Five Papers on the Archetypal*

Background of Family Psychology, ed., Patricia Berry (Dallas: Spring Publications, 1973), 79-92.

48. C.G. Jung, C.W. vol. 5, *Symbols of Transformation*, and vol. 14, *Mysterium Coniunctionis*.

49. Baird, *Category Formation*.

50. Richard Robinson, *Definition* (Oxford: At the Clarendon Press, 1965).

51. Ibid., 149.

52. Ibid.

53. Ibid., 152.

54. Ibid., 40.

55. Ibid., 16.

56. Ibid., 84.

57. Ibid., 66.

58. Baird, *Category Formation*, 7.

59. Ibid., 2.

60. Ibid., 2.

61. W. Richard Comstock, "Toward Open Definitions of Religion," *Journal of the American Academy of Religion* LII (September 1984): 504.

62. Baird, *Category Formation*, 18.

63. Paul Tillich, *Dynamics of Faith* (New York: Harper & Row, 1957), 11.

64. Baird, *Category Formation*, 18.

65. Comstock, 507.

66. Robert D. Baird, "Religion and the Legitimation of Nehru's Concept

of the Secular State," in *Religion and the Legitimation of Power in South Asia*, ed. Bardwell L. Smith (Leiden: E.J. Brill, 1978), 84.

67. Baird, *Category Formation*, 33.

68. Ibid., 25.

69. Mircea Eliade, *Patterns in Comparative Religion* (New York: World Publishing, 1972), 11.

70. Baird, *Category Formation*, 21.

71. George Williams, *The Quest for Meaning of Svami Vivekananda* (Chico, CA: New Horizons Press, 1974),6.

72. Ibid.

73. C.G. Jung, *Zwei Schriften über Analytische Psychologie*, Herausgeber: Marianne Hiehus-Jung, Lena Hurwitz-Eisner, Franz Riklin (Zürich: Rascher Verlag, 1964), 191.

74. Baird, *Category Formation*, 59.

75. Jung, C.W. 3, *The Psychogenesis of Mental Disease*.

76. Jolande Jacobi, *The Way of Individuation* (New York: Harcourt, Brace & World, 1967), preface.

77. I have adopted this classification scheme from George Williams' religio-historical study of Svami Vivekananda. It is extremely useful for ordering the diverse types of documentation I encountered in my study of Jung. See Williams, *The Quest for Meaning of Svami Vivekananda*, 7-8.

78. See Heisig, *Imago Dei*, page 147 for confirmation of this fact.

CHAPTER 2. PSYCHIC FRAGMENTATION

1. C.G. Jung, *Memories, Dreams, Reflections*, 84.

2. Ibid., 88.

3. C.G. Jung, The *Zofingia Lectures* (Princeton: Princeton University Press, 1983).

4. Carl Gustav Jung, *On the Psychology and Pathology of So-Called Occult Phenomena*, in C.W. 1, *Psychiatric Studies*.

5. C.G. Jung, *Zofingia Lectures*, 6.

6. Ibid.

7. Ibid., 45.

8. Ibid., 64. It also should be noted here that I have purposely omitted Jung's third lecture. That was his presidential acceptance speech and has no bearing on the present study.

9. Ibid., 65.

10. C.G. Jung, *On the Psychology and Pathology of So-called Occult Phenomena*, in C.W. 1:19.

11. Ibid., 53.

12. Ibid., 76.

13. Ibid., 79.

14. C.G. Jung, *Memories, Dreams, Reflections*, 114.

15. C.G. Jung, "On Hysterical Misreading," in C.W. 1:89-92.

16. Ibid., 91.

17. For the 1903 publication, see Jung's article, "On Simulated Insanity," in C.W. 1:159-187. For Jung's most important work on the association experiment, see "The Association of Normal Subjects," in C.W. 2, *Experimental Researches*, 3-196.

18. Jung, C.W. 2:3.

19. Ibid., 101.

20. Ibid.

21. Jung found that most of the associations of the epileptic patients were constellated by an illness complex. See C.G. Jung, "An Analysis of the Associations of an Epileptic," in C.W. 2:220.

22. C.G. Jung, "The Reaction-time Ratio in the Association Experiment," in C.W. 2:235.

23. C.G. Jung, "Cryptomnesia," in C.W. 1:98.

24. Jung, C.W. 2:245.

25. C.G. Jung, "Experimental Observations on the Faculty of Memory," in C.W. 2:272.

26. Ibid.

27. C.G. Jung, "Psychoanalysis and Association Experiments," in C.W. 2:288.

28. Ibid., 290.

29. C.G. Jung, "The Psychological Diagnosis of Evidence," in C.W. 2:316.

30. C.G. Jung, "The Psychopathological Significance of the Association Experiment," in C.W. 2:424.

31. C.G. Jung, "The Psychology of Dementia Praecox," in C.W. 3, *The Psychogenesis of Mental Disease*, 1-151. Ellenberger succinctly describes the differences between Jung's views on hysteria and dementia: "In hysteria Jung found that the associations were submerged by one great tenacious complex related to an old secret wound, but the individual could be cured if one could bring him to conquer and assimilate his complex. In dementia praecox, Jung found one or more fixed complexes no longer to be conquered." Henri Ellenberger, *The Discovery of the Unconscious*, 692.

32. Jung, C.W. 3:3.

33. Ibid., 18. For a good overview of the thought of Pierre Janet see Ellenberger, 331-417.

34. Jung, C.W. 3:36.

35. Ibid.

36. Jung, C.W. 3:41. Obviously, Jung had not yet formulated his conception of the self as the archetype of psychic unity.

37. Jung, C.W. 3:50. A later summary of the "complex" theory is given in "A Review of the Complex Theory," in C.W. 8, *The Structure and Dynamics of the Psyche,* 92-106.

38. Jung, C.W. 3:124.

39. Jung, *Memories, Dreams, Reflections,* 127.

40. Ibid.

41. Jung, C.W. 3:144. Jung continues his discussion of this point in "The Content of the Psychoses." See C.W. 3:153-178.

CHAPTER 3. PSYCHOANALYTIC INFLUENCE

1. C.G. Jung, "On Dreams," in C.W. 18, *The Symbolic Life,* 361-368.

2. William McGuire, ed., trans. Ralph Manheim and R.F.C Hull, *The Freud/Jung Letters.*

3. Peter Homans, *Jung in Context,* 47.

4. This work, originally published in German, contained articles by Jung and various other doctors. C.G. Jung, ed., *Diagnostische Assoziationsstudien: Beitrage zur experimentellen Psychopathologie* (Leipzig: Barth, 1906). For the English version of Jung's articles, see C.W. 2.

5. McGuire, 3.

6. Ibid., 4.

7. Ibid., 9.

8. Ibid., 11.

9. Ibid., 15.

10. Ibid., 19.

11. Ibid., 26.

12. Ibid., 78.

13. Ibid., 95.

14. Ibid., 341.

15. C.G. Jung, "Freud's Theory of Hysteria: A Reply to Aschaffenburg," in C.W. 4, *Freud and Psychoanalysis*, 4.

16. Ibid., 10.

17. Jung, "The Analysis of Dreams," in C. W. 4:25. Jung would eventually construct a dream theory of his own. In these early writings, though, he is still dependent on Freud's work in this area. For a summary of his latter views, see "On the Nature of Dreams," in C.W. 8, *The Structure and Dynamics of the Psyche*, 281-297.

18. Jung, C.W. 4:29.

19. Ibid. 56.

20. C.G. Jung, *Memories, Dreams, Reflections*, 158.

21. Ibid. Freud's biographer, Ernest Jones does not make reference to this statement. Although admitting that Freud and Jung did exchange dream interpretations, he seems to suggest that no problems arose in this regard. Ernest Jones, *The Life and Work of Sigmund Freud*, edited and abridged by Lionel Trilling and Steven Marcus, (New York: Basic Books, 1961), 266.

22. Jung, *Memories, Dreams, Reflections*, 158.

23. McGuire, 251.

24. Ibid., 258.

25. Ibid., 279.

26. Although agreeing with Homans in principle, I disagree with his

somewhat negative interpretation of this fact. For a discussion of his position see Homans, 58.

27. Jung, *Memories, Dreams, Reflections*, 158.

28. McGuire, 296.

29. Ibid., 308.

30. Ibid., 343.

31. Ibid., 344.

32. Ibid., 452.

33. C.G. Jung, *Psychology of the Unconscious*. The original German title was *Wandlungen und Symbole der Libido*.

34. McGuire, 509.

35. C.G. Jung, C.W. 5, *Symbols of Transformation*. My comments come from a 1927 reprint of the 1916 English edition. *Psychology of the Unconscious* (New York: Dodd, Mead and Company, 1927).

36. Jung, C.W. 5, preface xxiii.

37. Jung, *Psychology of the Unconscious*, 139.

38. Ibid., 144.

39. Ibid., 284.

40. Ibid., 335.

41. Ibid., 338-339. A useful summary of Jung's symbolic reinterpretation of incest and sacrifice is found in Aniela Jaffe, *Jung's Last Years*, 147-153.

42. Jung, *Psychology of the Unconscious*, 391.

43. Ibid., 434.

44. Ibid., 71.

45. Ibid., 76.

46. Ibid., 96.

47. Ibid., 262.

48. C.G. Jung, "The Theory of Psychoanalysis," in C.W. 4:83-226. Also see, Ellenberger, 697 for an overview of these talks.

49. Jung, C.W. 4:118.

50. Ibid., 163.

51. Carl Gustav Jung, "A Contribution to the Study of Psychological Types," in C.W. 6, *Psychological Types.*

52. Ibid., 509.

CHAPTER 4. THE UNCONSCIOUS AS LOCUS OF ULTIMACY

1. Aniela Jaffe, *Jung's Last Years*. In particular see chapter V, "The Creative Phases in Jung's Life."

2. Ibid., 155.

3. William McGuire, ed., trans., Ralph Manheim and R.F.C Hull, *The Freud/Jung Letters*, 551.

4. C.G. Jung, *Memories, Dreams, Reflections*, 171.

5. Ibid., 170.

6. Ibid., 194.

7. Ibid., 176.

8. Jaffe, 156.

9. C.G. Jung, *Memories, Dreams, Reflections*, 172.

10. Ibid., 179.

11. Ibid., 181.

12. Ibid., 182.

13. Ibid., 183.

14. Ibid., 185.

15. Ibid., 192.

16. The first article is entitled, "On Psychological Understanding," and is found in C.W. 3, *The Psychogenesis of Mental Disease*, 179.

17. Ibid., 181.

18. Ibid., 184-185.

19. Ibid., 189.

20. Peter Homans, *Jung in Context*, 80. Homans' view on this matter certainly seems to be in agreement with the description Jung gave concerning his state of mind at this time. In fact Jung goes so far as to indicate the psychotic-like nature of his experience. "In order to grasp the fantasies which were stirring in me underground, I knew that I had to let myself plummet down into them, as it were. I felt not only violent resistance to this, but a distinct fear. For I was afraid of losing command of myself and becoming prey to the fantasies—and as a psychiatrist I realized only too well what that meant." C.G. Jung, *Memories, Dreams, Reflections*, 178.

21. C.G Jung, "On the Importance of the Unconscious in Psychopathology," in C.W. 3:203.

22. Ibid., 206.

23. C.G. Jung, "The Transcendent Function," in C.W. 8, *The Structure and Dynamics of the Psyche*, 67-91.

24. Ibid., 69.

25. Ibid., 73.

26. Ibid., 84.

27. Ibid., 89.

28. Ibid., 88.

29. C.G. Jung, "The Conception of the Unconscious," in *Collected Papers on Analytical Psychology*, ed. Constance E. Long (London: Bailliere, Tindall and Cox, 1920), 445-474. This article is based on a lecture which Jung gave to the Zurich School for Analytical Psychology, 1916. In a much expanded and revised form it appeared as "The Relations between the Ego and the Unconscious," in C.W. 7, *Two Essays on Analytical Psychology* 123-244.

30. Ibid., 448.

31. Ibid., 452.

32. C.G. Jung, "Adaptation, Individuation, Collectivity," in C.W. 18, *The Symbolic Life* (Princeton: Princeton University Press, 1975), 449-454.

33. Ibid., 451.

34. Ibid.

35. Ibid., 452.

36. Ibid., 453.

37. Jung, "The Conception of the Unconscious," 466.

38. Ibid., 471.

39. C.G. Jung, "The Psychology of the Unconscious Processes," in *Collected Papers on Analytical Psychology*. This is a revised and expanded version of the 1912 article, "New Paths in Psychology." After further revisions, the 1917 version appeared as "On the Psychology of the Unconscious," in C.W. 7:9-119.

40. Ibid., 355.

41. Ibid., 380-381.

42. Ibid., 401.

43. Ibid., 391.

44. Ibid., 405.

45. C.G. Jung, C.W. 6, *Psychological Types.*

46. C.G. Jung, "The Psychology of the Unconscious Processes," 409.

47. Ibid.

48. Ibid., 411.

49. Ibid., 416.

50. Jung previously discussed the transcendent function in a 1916 article of the same name. See, "The Transcendent Function," in C.W. 8:67-91.

51. C.G. Jung, "The Psychology of the Unconscious Processes," 441.

52. Jung's interest in the problem of psychological types can be traced back to his 1913 article on this subject. See, "A Contribution to the Study of Psychological Types," in C.W. 6, *Psychological Types,* 499-509.

53. Jung, *Psychological Types,* 4.

54. Ibid., 450-451. For a further discussion of the type problem in general and the inferior infunction in particular, see Marie-Louise von Franz and James Hillman, *Jung's Typology* (Dallas: Spring Publications, 1971).

55. Jung, *Psychological Types,* 72.

56. Ibid., 75.

57. Ibid., 182.

58. Ibid., 263.

59. Ibid., 105.

60. Ibid., 58.

61. Jung's early references to Indian and Chinese thought are found in *Psychological Types*, 195-221. For an excellent secondary source on this subject, see Harold Coward, *Jung and Eastern Thought*.

62. Jung, *Psychological Types*, 212-213.

63. Ibid., 264.

64. Ibid., 108.

65. Ibid., 110.

66. Ibid., 112.

67. Ibid., 113.

68. Ibid., 266.

69. Ibid., 243.

70. Ibid., 248.

71. Ibid., 266.

CHAPTER 5. INDIVIDUATION OF THE SELF AS ULTIMATE CONCERN

1. C.G. Jung, "The Psychology of the Unconscious Processes," in *Collected Papers on Analytical Psychology*, 443-444.

2. C.G. Jung, C.W. 7, *Two Essays on Analytical Psychology*.

3. C.G. Jung, "New Paths in Psychology," in C.W. 7:245-268. And "The Psychology of the Unconscious Processes," in *Collected Papers on Analytical Psychology*.

4. Jung, *Two Essays on Analytical Psychology*, 3-119.

5. Ibid., 123-249.

6. C.G. Jung, C.W. 6, *Psychological Types*, 299.

7. C.G. Jung, "The Role of the Unconscious," in C.W. 10, *Civilization*

in Transition, 10. Note, however, that when conscious functioning is satisfactory, the influence of the unconscious diminishes.

8. Ibid., 15.

9. Jung, *Psychological Types*, 52.

10. C.G. Jung, "The Stages of Life," in C.W. 8, *The Structure and Dynamics of the Psyche*, 390.

11. With respect to the development of ego-consciousness, Jung gives the following explanation: "Only later, when the ego-contents—the so-called ego-complex—have acquired an energy of their own ... does the feeling of subjectivity or 'I-ness' arise. This may well be the moment when the child begins to speak of itself in the first person. The continuity of memory probably begins at this stage. Essentially, therefore, it would be a continuity of ego-memories." Ibid., 390.

12. Jung, *Psychological Types*, 425.

13. Jung, C.W. 7:174.

14. According to Jung, the self designates the entire range of psychic phenomena in humans. Hence its status as the archetype of unity of the entire personality. For an expanded definition of the self see Jung, C.W. 6:450.

15. Jung, C.W. 6:415.

16. Jung, C.W. 7:157.

17. Peter Homans, *Jung in Context*, 100.

18. In Jung's words, the persona is, "as its name implies, only a mask of the collective psyche, a mask that *feigns individuality*, making others and oneself believe that one is individual, whereas one is simply acting a role through which the collective psyche speaks." Jung, C.W. 7:157.

19. Ibid., 158.

20. Ibid.

21. Ibid., 145.

22. Ibid.

23. Concerning the repression of individuality, Jung writes: "A man cannot get rid of himself in favour of an artificial personality without punishment. Even the attempt to do so brings on, in all ordinary cases, unconscious reactions in the form of bad moods, affects, phobias, obsessive ideas, backslidings, vices, etc." Ibid., 194.

24. Ibid., 157.

25. Ibid.

26. Ibid., 158.

27. Ibid.

28. In the actual therapeutic setting, the analytical methods will vary from individual to individual, depending on the nature of the problem, and the stage of analysis. According to Jung: "Therapy is different in every case. . . . Psychotherapy and analysis are as varied as are human individuals. I treat every patient as individually as possible, because the solution of the problem is always an individual one." C.G. Jung, *Memories, Dreams, Reflections*, 131.

29. Jung, C.W. 7:160.

30. Ibid.

31. Jung likens this situation to the creation of a psychosis. "By bringing unconscious contents to the surface you artificially create a condition that bears the closest resemblance to a psychosis. The vast majority of mental illnesses (except those of a directly organic nature) are due to a disintegration of consciousness caused by the irresistible invasion of unconscious contents." C.G. Jung, "The Significance of the Unconscious in Individual Education," in C.W. 17, *The Development of Personality*, 153.

32. Jung, C.W. 7:162.

33. Homans, 99.

34. Jung, C.W. 7:163.

35. The crisis resulting from the ego's displacement is aptly summarized by the Jungian scholar, Murray Stein. "The 'I' 's standpoint is not fixed, and it occupies no clearly defined psychological location. It floats; it is not sharply delineated as 'this' and 'not that'; the boundaries between 'I' and 'not-I' blur and come much closer together than is true in the eras of fixed psychological identity.... The 'I' is not anchored to any particular inner images, ideas, or feelings. So, unattached, the 'I' floats and drifts and wanders across many former boundaries and forbidden frontiers." Murray Stein, *In Midlife* (Dallas: Spring Publications, 1983), 9.

36. Jung, C.W. 7:161.

37. Ibid., 163-171.

38. Ibid., 173.

39. Jung, C.W. 6:467-468. For a further overview and discussion of the anima see, James Hillman, *Anima* (Dallas: Spring Publications, 1985). Also, Emma Jung, *Animus and Anima* (Dallas: Spring Publications, 1981).

40. "If, therefore, we speak of the anima of a man, we must logically speak of the animus of a woman, if we are to give the soul of a woman its right name." Jung, C.W. 6:469.

41. C.G. Jung, "Marriage as a Psychological Relationship," in C.W. 17, *The Development of Personality*, 198.

42. Jung, C.W. 6:472. The role of the anima in relationships is discussed in Jung Singer, *Boundaries of the Soul*. In particular, see chapter 9. Also, John Sanford, *The Invisible Partners* (New York: Paulist Press, 1980).

43. Jung, C.W. 7:213.

44. Ibid., 201.

45. Ibid., 202.

46. Ibid., 217.

47. Ibid., 218.

48. Ibid., 224.

49. Ibid., 219.

50. Ibid., 227.

51. Ibid., 228.

52. Ibid.

53. Ibid., 235.

54. Ibid., 228-229.

55. Ibid., 230.

56. Ibid., 235.

57. Ibid., 230.

58. Jung describes this new psychic center in the following way. "If we picture the conscious mind, with the ego as its centre, as being opposed to the unconscious, and if we now add to our mental picture the process of assimilating the unconscious, we can think of this assimilation as a kind of approximation of conscious and unconscious, where the centre of the total personality no longer coincides with the ego, but with a point midway between the conscious and the unconscious. This would be the point of new equilibrium, a new centering of the total personality, a virtual centre which, on account of its focal position between conscious and unconscious, ensures for the personality a new and more solid foundation" C.W. 7:221.

59. Ibid., 238.

60. Ibid., 239.

61. With respect to the realization of the self, Jung writes: "I began to understand that the goal of psychic development is the self. There is no linear evolution; there is only a circumambulation of the self. Uniform development exists, at most, only at the beginning; later,

everything points toward the center." Jung, *Memories, Dreams, Reflections*, 196-197.

62. Jung, C.W. 6:448.

63. Jung, C.W. 8:60.

64. Jung, C.W. 7:225-226.

65. Ibid., 240.

66. Jung, *Memories, Dreams, Reflections*, 198-199.

67. Ibid. 197.

CHAPTER 6. SYMBOLS OF ULTIMACY

1. Barbara Hannah, *Jung: His Life and Work*, 191.

2. Henri F. Ellenberger, *The Discovery of the Unconscious*, 674-675.

3. For a description of Jung's impressions of India see, "The Dreamlike World of India," in C.W. 10, *Civilization in Transition*, 515-524; and "What India Can Teach Us," in C.W. 10:525-530.

4. Jung's writings on Eastern religions are found in C.W. 11, *Psychology and Religion: West and East*.

5. Jung's analysis of the events of World War II are contained in C.W. 10, section III.

6. Richard Wilhelm, trans., *The Secret of the Golden Flower* (London: Kegan Paul, Trench, Trubner & Co., 1931).

7. C.G. Jung, C.W. 13, *Alchemical Studies*, 3.
8. Wilhelm, 85.

9. Jung speaks of the counteraction of the unconscious to any conscious one-sidedness in Taoist terms. "When yang has reached its greatest strength, the dark power of yin is born within its depths; night begins at midday when yang breaks up and begins to change into yin." Ibid.

10. Ibid., 92.

11. Ibid., 96.

12. Ibid., 99.

13. Ibid., 123.

14. C.G. Jung, "Problems of Modern Psychotherapy," in C.W. 16, *The Practice of Psychotherapy*, 55.

15. Ibid., 59.

16. Ibid., 61-62.

17. Ibid., 65.

18. Ibid., 68.

19. Ibid., 75.

20. Jung sums up the relationship of affluence and meaninglessness: "Do not forget, however, that we are speaking not of people who still have to prove their social usefulness, but of those who can no longer see any sense in being socially useful and who have come upon the deeper and more dangerous question of the meaning of their own individual lives." C.G. Jung "The Aims of Psychotherapy," in C.W. 16:47-48.

21. C.G. Jung, "The Stages of Life," in C.W. 8, *The Structure and Dynamics of the Psyche*, 402-403.

22. C.G. Jung, "The Spriritual Problem of Modern Man," in C.W. 10:79.

23. Ibid., 83.

24. C.G. Jung, "Psychotherapists or the Clergy," in C.W. 11:327-347.

25. Ibid., 330-331.

26. Jung indicates that his patients' real concerns are of a religious nature. "Among all my patients in the second half of life . . . there has not been one whose problem in the last resort was not that of finding a

religious outlook on life. It is safe to say that every one of them fell ill because he had lost what the living religions of every age have given to their followers, and none of them has been really healed who did not regain his religious outlook. This of course has nothing whatever to do with a particular creed or membership of a church." Ibid., 334.

27. The goal of therapy, therefore, is to reestablish linkage with the unconscious. In Jung' s words: "To the patient it is nothing less than a revelation when something altogether strange rises up to confront him from the hidden depths of the psyche—something that is not his ego and is therefore beyond the reach of his personal will. He has regained access to the sources of psychic life, and this marks the beginning of the cure." Ibid., 345-346.

28. According to Jung: "This is brought about by the archetypes awaking to independent life and taking over the guidance of the psychic personality, thus supplanting the ego with its futile willing and striving." Ibid., 11:345.

29. C.G. Jung, "The Practical Use of Dream Analysis," in C.W. 16:160.

30. C.G. Jung, "The Development of Personality," in C.W. 17:167.

31. Ibid.

32. In addition, wholeness functions as Jung's ideal image of what it means to be human. "The fact is that the high ideal of educating the personality is not for children: for what is usually meant by personality—a well-rounded psychic whole that is capable of resistance and abounding in energy—is an *adult ideal.*" Ibid., 169.

33. Ibid., 171.

34. Ibid., 172.

35. Ibid., 173.

36. Jung summarizes the relationship between conventionality and wholeness: "The fact that the conventions always flourish in one form or another only proves that the vast majority of mankind do not choose their own way, but convention, and consequently develop not themselves but a method and a collective mode of life at the cost of their own wholeness." Ibid., 174.

37. Ibid., 175-176.

38. Jung suggests that there is an absoluteness about the laws of the psyche. "He has been called by that all-powerful, all-tyrannizing psychic necessity that is his own and his people's affliction. If he hearkens to the voice, he is at once set apart and isolated, as he has resolved to obey that law that commands him from within." Ibid., 178.

39. Ibid., 179.

40. C.G. Jung, "Some Aspects of Modern Psychotherapy," in C.W. 16:35.

41. Jung, C.W. 10:86. Elsewhere, Jung summarizes the unitary nature of the psyche: "And yet they are all our brothers, and in each of us there is at least one voice which seconds them, for in the end there is one psyche which embraces us all." Jung, C.W. 10:88

42. Jung, C.W. 17:186.

43. Carl G. Jung, "A Study in the Process of Individuation," in *The Integration of the Personality* (New York: Rarrar & Rinehart, Inc., 1939), 30-51; and C.G. Jung, "A Study in the Process of Individuation," in C.W. 9,i, *The Archetypes and the Collective Unconscious*, 290-354.

44. During this period Jung felt that Eastern philosophy presented a better picture of the psyche than anything found in the West. "It is obvious that this Western example of the process of individuation is far removed from the perfected beauty of Eastern symbols, like those of Laotse, which likewise give expression to this process, and at which the greatest masters have laboured. We Westerners, in spite of our so-called culture, are still barbarians and children when it comes to the psychic world. We have only just rediscovered the precious stone; we have still to polish it. We cannot yet compete with the intuitive clarity of Eastern vision." Jung, *The Integration of the Personality*, 41.

45. Jung, *The Integration of the Personality*, 38.

46. Concerning the importance of the unconscious, Jung writes: "Dealing with the unconscious has become a question of life for us. It is a matter of spiritual being or non-being." Ibid., 72.

47. C.G. Jung, "The Tavistock Lectures," in C.W. 18, *The Symbolic Life*, 1975.

48. Carl G. Jung, "Dream Symbols of the Process of Individuation," in *The Integration of the Personality*, 96-204. This article, after numerous revisions, formed part three of C.W. 12, *Psychology and Alchemy*.

49. Jung, *The Integration of the Personality*, 96.

50. Ibid., 120.

51. Ibid., 133.

52. Ibid.

53. Carl Gustav Jung, *Psychology and Religion* (New Haven: Yale University Press, 1972).

54. Ibid., 78.

55. Ibid., 82.

56. Concerning the center of the mandala, Jung writes: "The center is emphasized as a rule. But what we find there is a symbol of a very different meaning. It is a star, a sun, a flower, a cross of equal branches, a precious stone, a bowl filled with water or wine, a serpent coiled up, or a human being, but never a god." Ibid., 97.

57. Ibid., 98.

58. Ibid., 99.

59. Ibid.

60. Ibid., 102-103.

61. Ibid., 106.

62. Ibid., 105.

63. Ibid., 106.

64. C.G. Jung, "Conscious, Unconscious and Individuation," in C.W. 9,i: 275-289.

65. Ibid., 275.

66. C.G. Jung, "Forward to Suzuki's *Introduction to Zen Buddhism*," in C.W. 11:556.

67. C.G. Jung, "The Psychology of the Child Archetype," in C.W. 9, i:151-181.

68. Ibid., 162.

69. Ibid., 164.

70. Ibid., 166.

71. Ibid., 170-171.

72. Ibid., 171.

73. Here Jung explains the unity of psyche and world in physiological terms. "The deeper 'layers' of the psyche lose their individual uniqueness as they retreat farther and farther into darkness. 'Lower down,' that is to say as they approach the autonomous functional systems, they become increasingly collective until they are universalized and extinguished in the body's materiality, i.e., in chemical substances. The body's carbon is simply carbon. Hence 'at bottom' the psyche is simply 'world'." Ibid., 173.

74. Jung describes the attainment of wholeness as "a divine prerogative; an imponderable that determines the ultimate worth or worthlessness of a personality." Ibid., 179.

CHAPTER 7. ALCHEMY AND WHOLENESS

1. For a more detailed description of Jung's illness, see Barabara Hannah, *Jung: His Life and Work*, 276-277.

2. C.G. Jung, *Memories, Dreams, Reflections*, 289.

3. Ibid., 291.

4. Ibid.

5. Ibid., 292.

6. Ibid., 293.

7. Ibid., 295.

8. Henri F. Ellenberger, *The Discovery of the Unconscious*, 677.

9. Carl G. Jung, "Approaching the Unconscious," in *Man and His Symbols*, (New York: Dell Publishing, 1964).

10. Barbara Hannah, *Jung: His Life and Work*, 347.

11. For a good introduction to alchemy in general, and Jung's writings on alchemy in particular, see Marie-Louise von Franz, *Alchemy: An Introduction to the Symbolism and the Psychology* (Toronto: Inner City Books, 1980); and Marie-Louise von Franz, *Alchemical Active Imagination* (Irving, Texas: Spring Publications, 1979). For a discussion of the therapeutic significance of alchemy see the following works by James Hillman, "Alchemical Blue and the Unio Mentalis," *Sulfur* 1 (1981): 33-50; "Silver and the White Earth," *Spring* (1981): 21-28; and "The Therapeutic Value of Alchemical Language," *Dragonflies: Studies in Imaginal Psychology* I (1978): 33-42.

12. Jung, *Memories, Dreams, Reflections*, 204.

13. Ibid., 205.

14. Carl G. Jung, "Dream Symbols of the Process of Individuation," in *The Integration of the Personality*.

15. C.G. Jung, C.W. 12, *Psychology and Alchemy*.

16. C.G. Jung, "On the *Rosarium Philosophorum*," in C.W. 18, *The Symbolic Life*, 797-800.

17. C.G. Jung, "The Psychology of the Transference," in C.W. 16:163-323.

18. C.G. Jung, "Paracelsus," and "Paracelsus the Physician," in C.W. 15, *The Spirit in Man, Art, and Literature*.

19. C.G. Jung, "Paracelsus as a Spiritual Phenomenon," in C.W. 13, *Alchemical Studies*.

20. Jung, C.W. 12:228.

21. Ibid., 245.

22. C.G. Jung, C.W. 14, *Mysterium Coniunctionis*, 555-556.

23. Ibid., xiv.

24. Ibid., xv.

25. C.G. Jung, "The Spirit Mercurius," in C.W. 13:191-250.

26. Jung, C.W. 12:182.

27. Ibid., 228-232.

28. Jung, C.W. 16:163-323.

29. Ibid., 169.

30. Ibid., 185.

31. Ibid., 323.

32. Ibid., 208.

33. Ibid., 218.

34. Individuation, according to Jung, consists of two components: "in the first place it is an internal and subjective process of integration, and in the second it is an equally indispensable process of objective relationship." Ibid., 234.

35. Ibid., 235.

36. In another article, Jung emphasized the important role of psychotherapy in facilitating the developmental process: "I therefore consider it the prime task of psychotherapy today to pursue with singleness of purpose the goal of individual development. So doing, our efforts will follow nature's own striving to bring life to the fullest possible fruition in each individual, for only in the individual can life fulfil its meaning. . . ." Jung, C.W. 16:110.

37. Jung, C.W. 16:239.

38. The integration of the shadow means, according to Jung, that "wholeness is not so much perfection as completeness." Ibid., 239.

39. Ibid., 240.

40. Ibid., 250.

41. Ibid., 258.

42. Ibid., 265.

43. Ibid., 267.

44. Ibid.

45. Ibid., 279.

46. Concerning the intuition of wholeness Jung writes: "The imaginative activity of the fourth function—intuition, without which no realization is complete—is plainly evident in this anticipation of a possibility whose fulfilment could never be the object of empirical experience at all. . . . " Ibid., 281.

47. Ibid., 290-291.

48. Ibid., 293.

49. Ibid., 313-314.

50. Ibid., 200.

51. C.G. Jung, "Forward to a Catalogue on Alchemy," in C.W. 18:747.

52. Jung's book forewords written during this period, as well as most of his other forewords are found in C.W. 18.

53. Jung, C.W. 13:191-250.

54. Ibid., 232.

55. C.G. Jung, C.W. 9,ii, *Aion: Researches into the Phenomenology of the Self.*

56. Jung, C.W. 9,ii, 37.

57. Ibid. 31.

58. Ibid., 34. For a complete analysis of the evolution of the "god-image" in Jung' s writings, see James Heisig, *Imago Dei: A Study of C.G. Jung's Psychology of Religion.*

59. In Jung' s words: "Is the self a symbol of Christ, or is Christ a symbol of the self? In the present study I have affirmed the latter alternative. I have tried to show how the traditional Christ-image concentrates upon itself the characteristics of an archetype—the archetype of the self." Jung, C.W. 9,ii, 68.

60. For Jung's other writings on Christianity, see C.W. 11, *Psychology and Religion: West and East*, 107-470.

61. Jung, C.W. 12:1-38; and C.W. 13:251-349.

62. C.G. Jung, "The Visions of Zosimos," in C.W. 13:57-108.

63. Jung, C.W. 14:554.

64. Ibid., 3-41.

65. Ibid., 6.

66. Ibid., 42-88.

67. Ibid., 272.

68. Ibid., 330.

69. Ibid., 334.

70. Ibid., 355.

71. Jung explains that prior to the experience of unity one must confront the shadow. Viewed as the first stage of therapy, the confrontation with the shadow is typically a painful process. "Medical psychology has recognized today that it is a therapeutic necessity, indeed, the

first requisite of any thorough psychological method, for consciousness to confront its shadow. In the end this must lead to some kind of
union, even though the union consists at first in an open conflict, and
often remains so for a long time." Ibid., 365.

72. Jung describes the goal of the *unio mentalis* as follows. "The goal of
the procedure is the *unio mentalis,* the attainment of full knowledge
of the heights and depths of one's character." Ibid., 474.

73. Ibid., 476.

74. For an excellent discussion of the *unus mundus* and psyche/world
unity, see James Hillman, "Anima Mundi," *Spring* (1982); and Erich
Neumann, "The Psyche and the Transformation of the Reality Planes,"
Spring (1956): 81-111.

75. Jung, C.W. 14:533.

76. Ibid., 534.

77. Ibid., 540.

78. In the following quote Jung explicitly expresses the cosmic, unitary
nature of the self: "Not through me alone, but through all; for it is
not only the individual Atman-Purusha (Atman Brahman), the universal Atman, the pneuma, who breathes through all. We use the
word 'self' for this, contrasting it with the little ego. . . . What is
meant by the self is not only in me but in all beings, like the Atman,
like Tao. It is psychic "totality." C.G. Jung, "Good and Evil in Analytical Psychology," in C.W. 10:463.

79. Jung, C.W. 14:463.

80. Jung links up the self/world unity with the unus mundus in the
following statement. "With this conjecture of the identity of the
psyche and the physical we approach the alchemical view of the
unus mundus, the potential world of the first day of creation, when
there was as yet no second." Ibid., 537.

81. Ibid., 552.

82. Jung, *Memories, Dreams, Reflections,* 221.

CHAPTER 8. CONCLUSION

1. C.G. Jung, "The Relations between the Ego and the Unconscious," in C.W. 7, *Two Essays on Analytical Psychology*, 238.

2. C.G. Jung, "The Swiss Line in the European Spectrum," in C.W. 10, *Civilization in Transition*, 488.

3. C.G. Jung, C.W. 14, *Mysterium Coniunctionis*, 553.

4. Generally speaking, Jung saw his work as an antidote to the onesided conscious orientation of the contemporary world. "I have never counted upon any strong response, any powerful resonance, to my writings. They represent a compensation for our times, and I have been impelled to say what no one wants to hear. . . . I knew that what I said would be unwelcome, for it is difficult for people of our times to accept the counterweight to the conscious world. Jung, *Memories, Dreams, Reflections*, 222. Also see chapter six of the present study for further discussion of this point.

5. Jung himself gave a similar assessment of the stages of his work in his autobiography. There he states how his later writings were clarifications of the work that he began during his crisis years. "The years when I was pursuing my inner images were the most important in my life — in them everything essential was decided. It all began then; the later details are only supplements and clarifications of the material that burst forth from the unconscious, and at first swamped me. It was the *prima materia* for a lifetime's work." C.G. Jung, *Memories, Dreams, Reflections*, 199.

6. In his autobiography Jung summarizes the change that took place in his approach to the psyche as a result of his confrontation with the unconscious. "As a young man my goal had been to accomplish something in my science. But then, I hit upon this stream of lava, and the heat of its fires reshaped my life. That was the primal stuff which compelled me to work upon it, and my works are a more or less successful endeavor to incorporate this incandescent matter into the contemporary picture of the world." Jung, *Memories, Dreams, Reflections*, 199.

7. A full discussion of the individuation process during the formative phase of Jung's life is found in chapter five of the present study.

8. I have discussed Jung's alchemical writings in chapter seven, the "Late Years."

9. Jung, C.W. 14:546.

10. Ibid., 457-553. This work is discussed in chapter seven of the present study.

Select Bibilography

WORKS BY C.G. JUNG

Collected Works

The Collected Works of C.G. Jung. Bollingen Series XX, ed. by
Sir Herbert Read, Michael Fordham, Gerhard Adler. Trans.
by R.F.C. Hull. Princeton: Princeton University Press, 1953-
1979. 20 vols.
  Vol. 1: *Psychiatric Studies* (1957,1970).
  Vol. 2: *Experimental Researches,* trans. by Leopold
      Stein. (1973).
  Vol. 3: *The Psychogenesis of Mental Disease* (1960).
  Vol. 4: *Freud and Psychoanalysis* (1961).
  Vol. 5: *Symbols of Transformation* (1956,1962).
  Vol. 6: *Psychological Types* (1971).
  Vol. 7: *Two Essays on Analytical Psychology* (1953,
      1966).
  Vol. 8: *The Structure and Dynamics of the Psyche*
      (1960,1969).
  Vol. 9,i: *The Archetypes and the Collective Unconscious*
      (1959,1968).
  Vol. 9,ii: *Aion: Researches into the Phenomenology of
      the Self* (1959,1968).
  Vol. 10: *Civilization In Transition* (1964,1970).
  Vol. 11: *Psychology and Religion: West and East* (1958,
      1969).

Vol. 12: *Psychology and Alchemy* (1953,1968).
Vol. 13: *Alchemical Studies* (1967).
Vol. 14: *Mysterium Coniunctionis* (1963,1970).
Vol. 15: *The Spirit in Man, Art, and Literature* (1966).
Vol. 16: *The Practice of Psychotherapy* (1954,1966).
Vol. 17: *The Development of Personality* (1954).
Vol. 18: *The Symbolic Life* (1975).
Vol. 19: *General Bibliography* (1979).
Vol. 20: *General Index* (1979).

Articles and Books by C.G. Jung

For articles contained in the *Collected Works* (hereafter abbreviated as C.W.), I have included the date of publication and revisions after the title of the article.

"Adaptation, Individuation, Collectivity" (1916). In C.W. 18: 449-454.
"The Aims of Psychotherapy" (1931). In C.W. 16:36-52.
"The Analysis of Dreams" (1909). In C.W. 4:25-34.
"An Analysis of the Associations of an Epileptic" (1905). In C.W. 2:197-220.
"Approaching the Unconscious." In *Man and His Symbols*. Edited by Carl G. Jung, 1-94. New York: Dell Publishing, 1964.
"The Association of Normal Subjects" (1904). In C.W. 2:3-196.
"Commentary on *The Secret of the Golden Flower*" (1929). In C.W. 13:1-56.
"The Conception of the Unconscious." In *Collected Papers on Analytical Psychology*. Edited by Constance E. Long, 445-474. London: Bailliere, Tindall and Cox, 1920.
"Conscious, Unconscious, and Individuation" (1939). In C.W. 9,i:275-289.
"The Content of the Psychoses" (1908/1914). In C.W. 3:153-178.
"A Contribution to the Study of Psychological Types" (1913). In C.W. 6:499-509.
"Cryptomnesia" (1905). In C.W. 1:95-106.
"The Development of Personality" (1934). In C.W. 17:165-186.
Diagnostische Assoziationsstudien: Beitrage zur experimentellen Psychopathologie. Leipzig: Barth, 1906.
"Dream Symbolism of the Process of Individuation" (1936). *In*

Integration of the Personality, 96-204. New York: Rarrar & Rinehart, 1939.

"The Dreamlike World of India" (1939). In C.W. 10:515-524.

"Experimental Observations on the Faculty of Memory" (1905). In C.W. 2:272-287.

"Forward to a Catalogue on Alchemy" (1946). In C.W. 18:747.

"Forward to Suzuki's *Introduction to Zen Buddhism*" (1939). In C.W. 11:538-557.

"Freud's Theory of Hysteria: A Reply to Aschaffenburg" (1906). In C.W. 4:3-9.

"Good and Evil in Analytical Psychology" (1959). In C.W. 10:456-468.

"Marriage as a Psychological Relationship" (1925). In C.W. 17:187-201.

Memories, Dreams, Reflections, ed. Aniela Jaffe. New York: Vintage Books, 1965.

"New Paths in Psychology" (1912). In C.W. 7:245-268.

"On Hysterical Misreading" (1904). In C.W. 1:89-92.

"On Psychological Understanding" (1914). In C.W. 3:179-193.

"On Simulated Insanity" (1903). In C.W. 1:159-187.

"On the Importance of the Unconscious in Psychopathology (1914). In C.W. 3:203-210.

"On the Nature of Dreams" (1945/1948). In C.W. 8:281-297.

On the Psychology and Pathology of So-Called Occult Phenomena (1902). In G.W. 1:3-88.

"On the Psychology of the Unconscious" (1917/1926/1943). In C.W. 7:1-119.

"On the Rosarium Philosophorum" (1937). In C.W. 18:797-800.

"Paracelsus" (1929). In C.W. 15:3-12

"Paracelsus the Physician" (1941). In C.W. 15:13-30.

"The Practical Use of Dream-Analysis" (1934). In C.W. 16:139-161.

"Problems of Modern Psychotherapy" (1929). In C.W. 16:53 75.

"Psychoanalysis and Association Experiments" (1906). In C.W. 2:288-317.

"The Psychological Diagnosis of Evidence" (1906). In C.W. 2:318-352.

Psychology and Religion (1937). New Haven: Yale University Press, 1972.

The Psychology of Dementia Praecox (1907). In C.W. 3:1-151.
"The Psychology of the Child Archetype" (1940). In C.W. 9,i:151-181.
The Psychology of the Transference (1946). In C.W. 16:163-321.
Psychology of the Unconscious. New York: Moffat, Yard, 1916.
"The Psychology of the Unconscious Processes" (1917). In *Collected Papers on Analytical Psychology.* Edited by Constance E. Long, 354-444. London: Bailliere, Tindall and Cox, 1920.
"The Psychopathological Significance of the Association Experiment" (1906). In C.W. 2:408-425.
"Psychotherapists or the Clergy" (1932). In C.W. 11:327-347.
"Psychotherapy Today" (1945). In C.W. 16:94-110.
"The Reaction-time Ratio in the Association Experiment" (1905). In C.W. 2:221-271.
"The Relations between the Ego and the Unconscious" (1928). In C.W. 7:121-241.
"A Review of the Complex Theory" (1934). In C.W. 8:92-104.
"The Role of the Unconscious" (1918). In C.W. 10:3-28.
"The Significance of the Unconscious in Individual Education" (1928). In C.W. 17:149-164.
"Some Aspects of Modern Psychotherapy" (1930). In C.W. 16:29-35.
"The Spirit Mercurius" (1943/1948). In C.W. 13:191-200.
"The Spiritual Problem of Modern Man" (1928/1931). In C.W. 10:74-94.
"The Stages of Life" (1930). In C.W. 8:387-403.
"A Study in the Process of Individuation" (1934/1950). In C.W. 9,i:290-354.
"A Study in the Process of Individuation." *In Integration of the Personality*, 30-51. New York: Rarrar & Rinehart, 1939. This is the original version of the article of the same title revised and published in the *Collected Works.*
"The Swiss Line in the European Spectrum" (1928). In C.W. 10:479-488.
"The Tavistock Lectures" (1935). In C.W. 18:1-182.
"The Theory of Psychoanalysis" (1913). In C.W. 4:83-226.
"The Transcendent Function" (1916/1957). In C.W. 8:67-91.
"The Visions of Zosimos" (1938/1954). In C.W. 13:57-108.
Wandlungen und Symbole der Libido. Leipzig and Vienna: Franz

Deuticke, 1912.
"What India Can Teach Us" (1939). In C.W. 10:525-530.
The Zofingia Lectures. Princeton: Princeton University Press, 1983. (Delivered between the years 1896-1899.)
Zur Psychologie und Pathologie sogenannter occulter Phänomene. Leipzig: Oswald Mutze, 1902.
Zwei Schriften über Analytische Psychologie. Herausgeber: Marianne Hiehus-Jung, Lena Hurwitz-Eisner, Franz Riklin. Zurich: Rascher Verlag, 1964.

Interpretive Works

Adler, Gerhard. "C.G. Jung's Contribution to Modern Consciousness." *British Journal of Medical Psychology* 20 (1945): 207-220.
Baird, Robert D. *Category Formation and the History of Religions.* The Hague: Mouton, 1971.
———. "Religion and the Legitimation of Nehru's Concept of the Secular State." In *Religion and the Legitimation of Power in South Asia,* ed. Bardwell L. Smith, 73-87. Leiden: E.J. Brill, 1978.
Bodkin, Maud. *Archetypal Patterns In Poetry.* London: Oxford University Press, 1934.
Broom, Vincent. *Jung.* New York: Atheneum, 1978.
Browning, Don S. *Religious Thought and the Modern Psychologies.* Philadelphia: Fortress Press, 1987.
Clift, Wallace B. *Jung and Christianity: The Challenge of Reconciliation.* New York: Crossroad, 1982.
Comstock, W. Richard "Toward Open Definitions of Religion." *Journal of the American Academy of Religion* LII/3 (1984): 499-517.
Coward, Harold. *Jung and Eastern Thought.* Albany: State University of New York Press, 1985.
Cox, David. *Jung and Saint Paul.* New York: Association Press, 1959.
Dourley, John P. *The Illness that We Are: A Jungian Critique of Christianity.* Toronto: Inner City Books, 1984.
———. *The Psyche as Sacrament: C.G. Jung and Paul Tillich.* Toronto: Inner City Books, 1981.

Edinger, Edward. *Ego and Archetype: Individuation and the Religious Function of the Psyche.* New York: Penguin Books, 1972.

Eliade, Mircea. *Patterns in Comparative Religion.* New York: World Publishing, 1972.

Ellenberger, Henri F. *The Discovery of the Unconscious.* New York: Basic Books, 1970.

Fordham, Michael. "The Evolution of Jung's Researches." *British Journal of Medical Psychology* 29 (1956): 3-8.

Franz, Marie-Louise von. *Alchemical Active Imagination.* Irving, Texas: Spring Publications, 1979.

_____ . *Alchemy: An Introduction to the Symbolism and the Psychology.* Toronto: Inner City Books, 1980.

_____ . *C.G. Jung: His Myth in Our Time.* New York: G.P. Putnam's Sons, 1975.

_____ . *An Introduction to the Interpretation of Fairy-Tales.* New York: Spring Publications, 1970.

_____ . "The Process of Individuation." *In Man and His Symbols*, ed. C.G. Jung, 157-254. New York: Dell Publishing, 1964.

Franz, Marie-Louise von, and James Hillman. *Jung's Typology.* Dallas: Spring Publications, 1971.

Goldbrunner, Josef. *Individuation.* Notre Dame: University of Notre Dame Press, 1964.

Hall, Calvin, and Vernon Nordby. *A Primer of Jungian Psychology.* New York: Mentor, 1973.

Hannah, Barbara. *Jung: His Life and Work.* New York: G.P. Putnam's Sons, 1976.

_____ . *Striving towards Wholeness.* New York: G.P. Putnam's Sons, 1971.

Heisig, James. *Imago Dei: A Study of C.G. Jung's Psychology of Religion.* London: Associated University Presses, 1979.

Hillman, James. "Alchemical Blue and the Unio Mentalis." *Sulfur* 1 (1981): 33-50.

_____ . *Anima.* Dallas: Spring Publications, 1985.

_____ . "Anima Mundi." *Spring* (1982): 71-93.

_____ . "The Great Mother, Her Son, Her Hero, and the Puer." In *Fathers and Mothers: Five Papers on the Archetypal Background of Family Psychology*, ed. Patricia Berry, 79-92.

Dallas: Spring Publications, 1973.

_____ . "Silver and the White Earth." *Spring* (1981): 21-28.

_____ . "The Therapeutic Value of Alchemical Language." *Dragonflies: Studies in Imaginal Psychology* 1 (1978): 33-42.

Homans, Peter. *Jung in Context.* Chicago: The University of Chicago Press, 1979.

Jacobi, Jolande. *Der Weg zur Individuation.* Zurich: Rascher, 1965.

_____ . *The Way of Individuation.* New York: Harcourt, Brace & World, 1967.

Jaffe, Aniela. *Jung's Last Years.* Dallas: Spring Publications, 1984.

Jones, Ernest. *The Life and Work of Sigmund Freud.* Edited and abridged by Lionel Trilling and Steven Marcus. New York: Basic Books, 1961.

Jung, Emma. *Animus and Anima.* Dallas: Spring Publications, 1981.

Katz, Nathan, ed. *Buddhist and Western Psychology.* Boulder: Prajna Press, 1983.

Kelsey, Morton. *Christo-Psychology.* New York: Crossroad Publishing Company, 1982.

Lambert, Kenneth. "Jung's Later Work." *Journal of the American Psychoanalytic Association* X (1962): 191-197.

Lewis, Aubrey. "Jung's Early Work." *The Journal of Analytical Psychology* 11 (1957): 119-136.

Mattoon, Mary Ann. *Jungian Psychology in Perspective.* New York: The Free Press, 1981.

May, Gerald, G. *Will & Spirit: A Contemplative Psychology.* New York: Harper & Row, 1982.

McGuire, William, ed. *The Freud/Jung Letters.* Princeton: Princeton University Press, 1974.

Neumann, Erich. "The Psyche and the Transformation of the Reality Planes." *Spring* (1956): 81-111.

Rieff, Philip. *The Triumph of the Therapeutic.* New York: Harper & Row, 1966.

Robinson, Richard. *Definition.* Oxford: At the Clarendon Press, 1965.

Sanford, John. *The Invisible Partners.* New York: Paulist Press, 1980.

Singer, June. *Boundaries of the Soul.* Garden City, New York:

Doubleday Publishing, 1972.

Stein, Murray. *In Midlife*. Dallas: Spring Publications, 1983.

———, ed. *Jungian Analysis*. Boulder: Shambhala, 1984.

Stern, Paul. *C.G. Jung: The Haunted Prophet*. New York: George Braziller, Inc., 1976.

Storr, Anthony. *C.G. Jung*. New York: Viking Press, 1973.

Tillich, Paul. *Dynamics of Faith*. New York: Harper & Row, 1957.

Van der Post, Laurens. *Jung and the Story of Our Time*. New York: Random House, 1977.

Vincie, Joseph, and Margreta Rathbauer-Vincie. *C.G. Jung and Analytical Psychology: A Comprehensive Bibliography*. New York: Garland Publishing, 1977.

Welch, John. *Spiritual Pilgrims: Carl Jung and Teresa of Avila*. New York: Paulist Press, 1982.

Whitmont, Edward C. *The Symbolic Quest*. Princeton: Princeton University Press, 1969.

Wilhelm, Richard, trans. *The Secret of the Golden Flower*. London: Kegan Paul, Trench, Trubner & Co., 1931.

Williams, George. *The Quest for Meaning of Svami Vivekananda*. Chico, CA: New Horizons Press, 1974.

Index

(Items appearing in the footnotes and bibliography are not included in the index).